Fashionable Lace

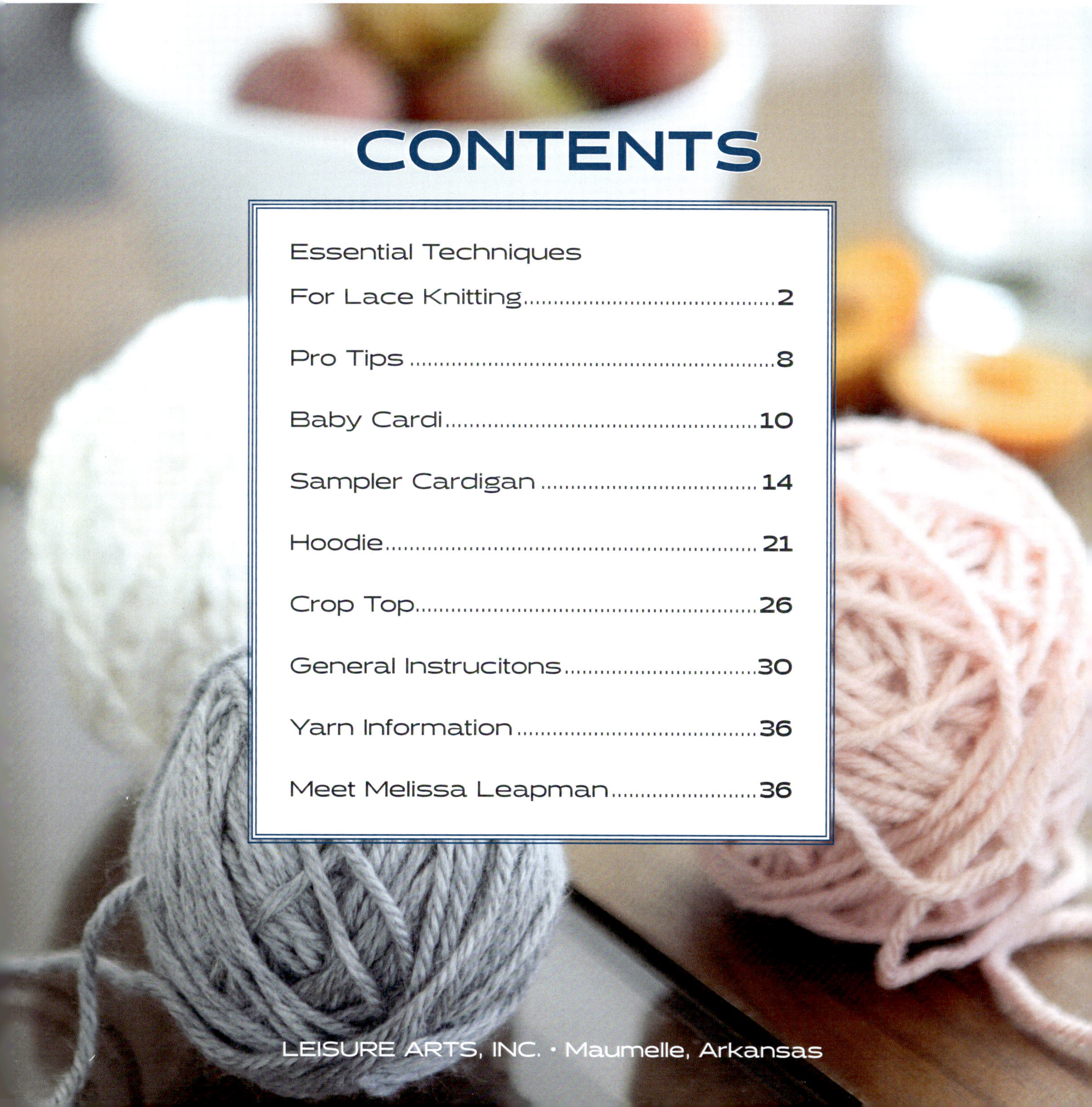

CONTENTS

Essential Techniques For Lace Knitting....2

Pro Tips....8

Baby Cardi....10

Sampler Cardigan....14

Hoodie....21

Crop Top....26

General Instrucitons....30

Yarn Information....36

Meet Melissa Leapman....36

LEISURE ARTS, INC. • Maumelle, Arkansas

Essential Techniques For Lace Knitting

Lace is one of those cool knitting techniques that looks much more complicated than it is. These openwork patterns and motifs are created simply by adding holes to a solid fabric!

MATERIALS

Lace knitting doesn't require any special materials, however following are some things to make learning and knitting these special fabrics super easy and fun.

Yarn

Nearly any yarn can be used for lace knitting. Traditionally, fine yarns were used, but using thicker yarns, even super chunky weight, yields a more modern-looking fabric with lots of pop.

Smooth yarns work best, since they allow the beautiful stitchwork to shine. I stay away from most novelty yarns such as eyelash, thick-and-thin yarn, and tweeds for this reason.

Needles

Obviously, any type of knitting needle works for lace, but since you'll be doing lots of decreases, the pointier the tip, the better. That makes it easier to get the tip into two or three stitches at once. Believe it or not, every manufacturer's needle tips have a unique shape. Choose the ones that work best for you.

Another thing to consider is the material used to make your knitting needles. For beginners, I always recommend wood or bamboo tools. These needles are slightly sticky and make it easier to avoid dropping stitches, the bane of every knitter's existence.

Not that knitting is a race, but for speed knitting, metal needles are useful. Their slippery surface allows stitches to glide quickly and easily.

Plastic or resin needles work universally because they're neither too "grabby" nor too slick. I always have a set of plastic interchangeable needles in my project bag.

The type of project you're knitting will determine whether your needles should be straight or circular. When knitting in the round, you'll use circular needles, of course. But for flat projects that call for a large number of stitches, a long circular needle is best. In this case, don't join at the end of the rows; instead, just work back and forth in rows. The flexible needle accommodates the large number of stitches.

GAUGE

Gauge refers to the number of stitches and rows per inch in your knitted fabric, and it depends on the size of each individual stitch. It is essential to understand how gauge works in order to control the finished size of your knitted projects.

Many things affect the size of your stitches, from the size of your yarn to the size of your needles, to the material your needles are made of. Even your mood can affect your gauge: knitting nervously during a horror movie will likely result in a tighter gauge than knitting while relaxing in front of a fireplace on vacation.

Commercial patterns, including those in this book, are written for a particular gauge. If you want your finished project to be the same size as the one listed in the Finished Measurements section of the pattern (and fit like the project photographed), be sure to match the gauge called for exactly. Even the difference of one-half of a stitch per inch could make your piece several inches larger or smaller than you expect. (Ask me how I know!) You might have to knit several gauge swatches using different needle sizes to obtain the perfect gauge. Don't skip this crucial step! Remember: any knitting time is fun! Even swatch knitting!

Typically, patterns will indicate the desired gauge over four inches rather than over one inch. Measuring over a larger width yields a more accurate determination of the gauge of the fabric since individual stitches tend to vary slightly in size, even for the most experienced knitters.

If you find it difficult to measure your gauge in a fabric worked in a pattern stitch such as lace, cast on a few repeats of the pattern and work for about six inches and then bind off. It'll be easy to measure the width and height of one stitch repeat, and you can use that information to determine how many stitches you have per inch.

If you plan to block your finished pieces ***(page 7)***, be sure to block your gauge swatches as well. As it refines the fabric and makes your stitches look uniform, it also changes the size and shape of stitches, affecting the gauge.

To accurately measure your gauge, knit a gauge swatch in the stitch pattern used for the project, bind off all stitches, and then use rust-proof pins (trust me!) to secure the fabric to a flat surface (blocking mats or a folded-up bath towel will work). Be sure that your piece of knitted fabric is at least 5" (12.5 cm) square, since you will want to avoid the edge stitches on all sides of the fabric when measuring. These edge stitches, called selvage stitches, tend to be wonky and uneven in size and are not representative of most of your fabric. Besides, they will be hidden within the seams (if any) of your project and will not affect its finished measurements.

Count the number of stitches over 4" (10 cm), staying away from all edges of the fabric, and avoid pressing down too hard on the fabric.

If you have fewer stitches per inch than what is called for in the pattern, knit another swatch with smaller knitting needles; if you have more stitches, then try again with larger ones. When knitting, it doesn't matter what size knitting needles you use, only that your gauge matches the one called for in the pattern.

BEGINNING AND ENDING LACE

Since lace projects are often blocked when completed, it is important to have relatively loose cast on and bind off edges. Here are some of my favorite methods.

Simple Cast On

To achieve a stretchy cast on I usually just use larger needles (up one or two sizes) with my regular cast on technique, long tail or knit on. The larger needles allow for extra give when blocking ***(see page 7)***.

Beginning Ring

I use this method when casting on just a few stitches in the round. It's great because it makes it so easy to neatly tighten the center hole.

Here's how: Make a loop in the yarn, keeping the working yarn from the ball on top and a 6" (15 cm) tail underneath ***(Photo A)***. ★ Insert a crochet hook in the center of the loop, then use it to reach up and grab the working yarn coming out of the ball ***(Photo B)***. Draw the working yarn through the middle of the loop ***(Photo C)***, then wrap the yarn around the hook once more and draw it through the loop on the hook ***(Photo D)***. Repeat from the ★ as many times as necessary to cast on the specified number of stitches ***(Photo E)***. Distribute these stitches onto double-pointed needles or a circular needle to begin knitting. Finally, tug on the yarn tail to tighten the loop.

Super Stretchy Bind Off

This technique leaves an elastic edge that's perfect for projects that will be blocked.

Here's how: K2, ★ return the 2 sts back to the left needle, K2 tog tbl ***(Photo F)***, K1; repeat from ★ across until all sts have been bound off.

Photo A

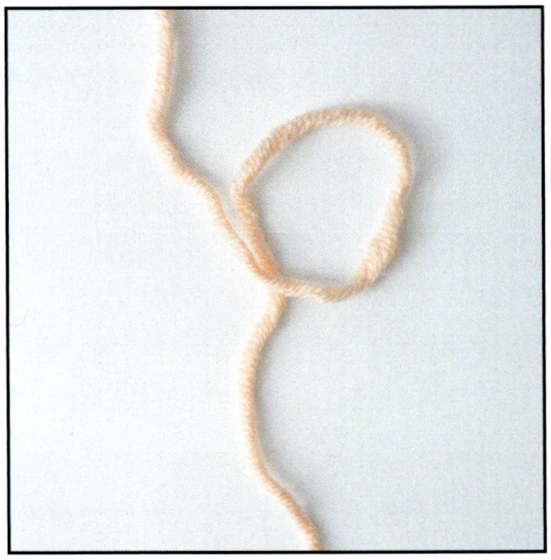

Photo B

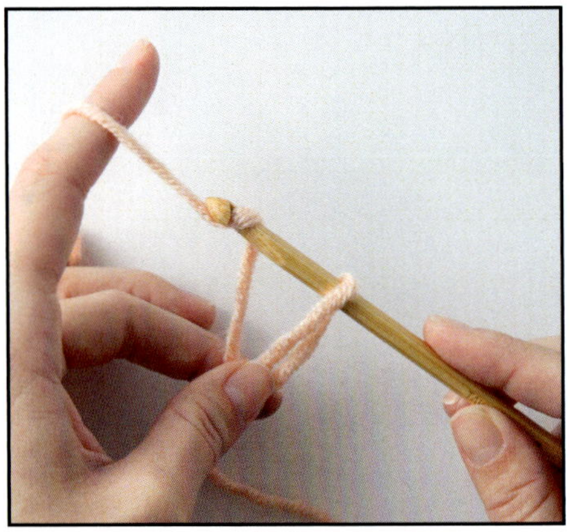

Photo C

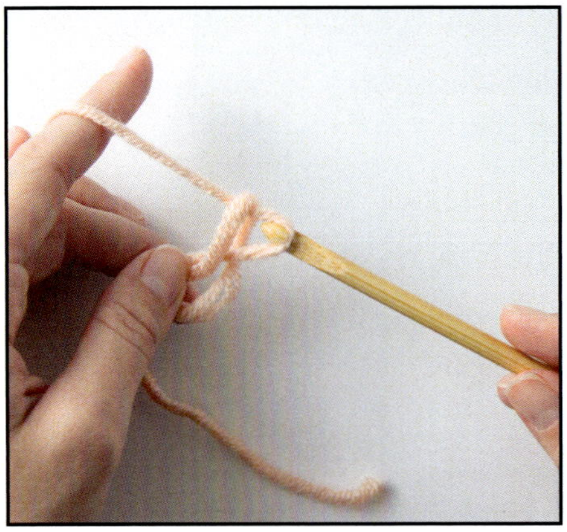

Photo D

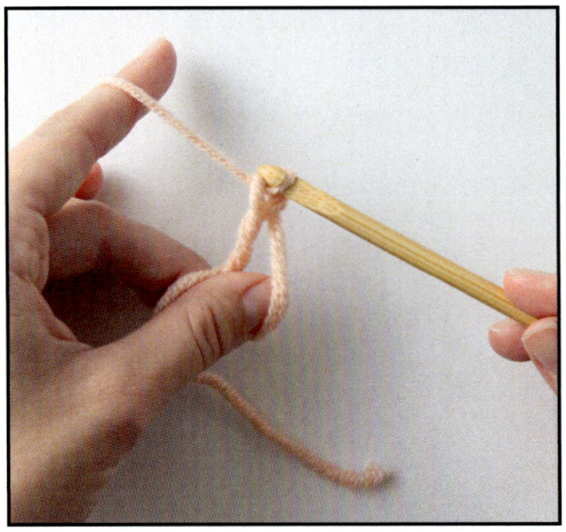

Photo E

Photo F

LACE CONSTRUCTION

Lace designs use yarn over stitches to intentionally add delicate holes to the fabric. When knitting these openwork patterns, YO increases are balanced with decreases in order to keep the stitch count constant. As intricate as some lace patterns might appear, they're relatively easy to knit! (Sssshhhhhh. Let's keep that secret just between us!)

The increases are predominately YO stitches; the decreases are usually knit two together ***(abbreviated K2 tog)*** and slip slip knit ***(abbreviated SSK)***. These decreases are perfect mirror images of each other and are the secret to the lovely patternwork.

Here are the increases and decreases you will encounter in lace knitting.

Increases

To make a yarn over between two knit stitches: The working yarn is in the **back**. Bring it between the two needle tips to the **front** ***(Photo G)***. As you knit the next stitch, the yarn will go over the right-hand needle, creating the yarn over.

To make a yarn over between a knit and a purl stitch: The working yarn is in the **back**. Bring it between the two needle tips to the **front**, and then wrap it all the way around the right-hand needle to the **front** again ***(Photo H)***.

To make a yarn over between a purl and a knit stitch: The working yarn is in the front. As you knit the next stitch, the yarn will go over the right-hand needle, creating the yarn over ***(Photo I)***.

To make a yarn over between two purl stitches: The working yarn is in the **front**. Wrap it all the way around the right-hand needle to the **front** creating the yarn over ***(Photo J)***.

Decreases

To knit two together *(abbreviated K2 tog)*: With the working yarn in the **back**, insert the tip of the right-hand needle into two stitches **at once** as if to **knit** ***(Photo K)***. Wrap the yarn around to complete the stitch as a knit stitch. *This decrease slants to the right.*

Photo G

Photo H

Photo I

Photo J

Photo K

To slip, slip, knit *(abbreviated SSK)*: With the working yarn in the **back**, insert the right-hand needle from the left to the right (knitwise), into the first and second stitches on the left needle, *one at a time*, and slip them onto the right needle ***(Photo L)***. Then, insert the tip of the left-hand needle into the **front** of both slipped stitches ***(Photo M)*** and knit them together from this position, through their back loops. *This decrease slants to the left.*

To knit three stitches together *(abbreviated K3 tog)*: With the working yarn in the **back**, insert the tip of the right-hand needle into three stitches **at once** as if to **knit**. Complete the same as a K2 tog. *This double decrease slants to the right.*

To slip, slip, slip, knit *(abbreviated SSSK)*: With the working yarn in the **back**, insert the right-hand needle from the left to the right (knitwise), into the first, second and third stitches on the left needle, *one at a time*, and slip them onto the right needle. Complete same as a SSK. *This double decrease slants to the left.*

To make a slip two together, knit one, pass two slipped stitches over *(abbreviated S2KP2)*: With the working yarn in the **back**, insert the right-hand needle into the next 2 stitches **at once** as if to do a K2 tog, and slip them onto the right-hand needle ***(Photo N)***. Knit the next stitch the regular way, then pass the 2 slipped stitches over the stitch you just knitted ***(Photo O)***. *This double decrease is vertical and has no slant* ***(Photo P)***.

Photo L

Photo M

Photo N

Photo O

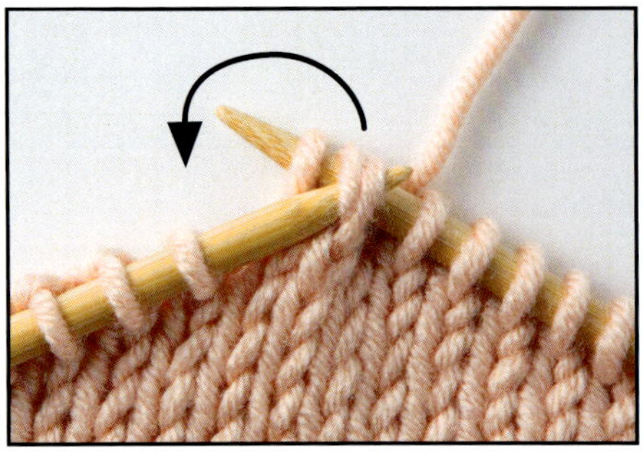

Photo P

Slanted Decreases

If you find it difficult to remember which decrease leans to the left and which one leans to the right you're not alone! Here's an easy way to keep them straight:

Write out the abbreviated names of the decreases "K2 tog" and "SSK". Then, draw a diagonal line through the right slant of the "2" and through the left slant of the "s" as shown.

The K2 tog leans to the right and the SSK leans to the left. Easy!

k2tog
(slants to the right)

ssk
(slants to the left)

FINISHING TECHNIQUES

After all the knitting is completed, good finishing techniques will ensure that your project will look perfect.

Blocking

Blocking is a finishing process that helps "set" any knitted project to your desired size. It evens out the stitches, magically making the overall fabric look uniformly knit. In lace projects, blocking opens up the fabric, making it airy and beautiful, emphasizing the patternwork. Knitters have several methods of blocking, but wet-blocking is the one I like best.

To do: Launder the knitted piece, being sure to follow the manufacturer's instructions on the yarn label. Lay the piece flat on a padded surface out of direct sunlight, patting it gently to your desired measurements. Using rust-proof pins, pin the damp fabric down and allow it to dry completely.

Dealing With Yarn Ends

Yarn tails are a necessary evil in knitting. Here's how to take care of them so they are invisible and secure.

Use a pointed-end yarn needle to make short running stitches on the **wrong** side of your fabric in a diagonal line for about 1" (2.5 cm) or so, piercing the yarn strands that comprise the stitches of your fabric. Then, work back again to where you began, working alongside your previous running stitches. Finally, to secure the tail, work a stitch or two and actually pierce the stitches you just created. Be sure to work each tail individually, in opposite diagonal directions, and you will secure your yarn ends while keeping the public side of your fabric beautiful.

Pro Tips

for Knitting from Charts

- Use a sticky note to help keep track of where you are on the chart. Place it above the row you are working and move it up after you complete each row.
- Place markers on the knitting needle after each stitch repeat; it'll make it easy to count your stitches.
- Use a highlighter to color in each wrong side row. This will be a visual clue that the symbols on these rows must be mentally reversed when knitting.

LACE CHARTS 101

While I've included all patterns in this book in both text and chart form, I encourage you to try to wean yourself off the written-out versions. Once you get accustomed to using them, knitting charts can make your stitching easier, faster, and more fun.

How They Work

Knitting charts are a visual representation of the public side of knitted fabric.

Each square of the grid corresponds to one stitch and each row of squares corresponds to one row (or round) of stitches.

Charts are read in the same way that the fabric is knit: from the lower edge up, with the first row at the bottom of the chart and the last row at the top.

Right side rows are read from **right** to **left**, in the same order that stitches present themselves to you on the left-hand knitting needle.

At the end of this first row, you flip your knitting before starting the next row, and the **wrong** side of the fabric faces you. Physically, the first stitch of this **wrong** side row is the same stitch as the last stitch of the right-side row you just completed. Thus, **wrong side** rows on charts are read in the opposite direction, from **left** to **right**.

Note: When working in the round rather than back and forth in rows, the right side of the fabric is always facing you, so **all** rows of the chart are read from **right** to **left**.

Charts make it easy to see how many stitches are involved in a pattern. In some charts, a bold box sets off the stitch repeat, and if extra stitches are required on each side to center the pattern on the fabric, they are shown to the left and right of the repeat. In the *Sampler Cardigan* on page 14, for example, the Second Lace Section pattern on page 16 has a multiple of six stitches plus one stitch; it is a six-stitch repeat with one "balancing" stitch on the right-hand side. This stitch sits outside the stitch repeat and so is worked once per row. It is the first stitch of every right side row, and since wrong side rows are read from left-to-right, it is the last stitch of these rows.

Symbols

Each symbol on a chart indicates the way a stitch will be worked, and the arrangement of the symbols on the chart determines the stitch pattern.

Usually, the symbols visually resemble the way the resulting stitches will appear on the public side of the knitted fabric. The symbol for a knit stitch, for example, is a blank box, mimicking the flat appearance of the knit stitch itself; the dot symbol for a purl stitch depicts the bumpy appearance of a purled stitch. *Refer to the symbol key near each chart for easy translation.*

All symbols are shown in charts as they appear on the public side of the fabric. This means that the same symbol means different things on **right** and **wrong** side rows. The blank box, for instance, represents a knit stitch on a **right** side row, but if you're on a **wrong** side row and want the stitch to appear as a knit stitch on the reverse side of the fabric, you must purl it.

Often, wrong side rows are pretty simple: you just knit the knit stitches and purl the purl stitches and YO stitches as they present themselves to you on the knitting needle. Scan the entire chart before you begin knitting to confirm that this is the case. If so, you can zip along those "rest rows" reading your knitting rather than the chart!

Projects

Here are 4 lace projects to practice and showcase your new skills ***(pages 10-29)***. Makers gotta make!

Baby Cardi

●●○○ EASY

SHOPPING LIST

Yarn (Medium Weight) MEDIUM 4

[7 ounces, 370 yards
(198 grams, 338 meters) per skein]:

- ☐ 1 skein

Knitting Needles

29" (73.5 cm) Circular,

- ☐ Size 8 (5 mm)
  or size needed for gauge

Double-pointed needles (set of 5),

- ☐ Size 8 (5 mm) for Sleeves

Additional Supplies

- ☐ Stitch markers
- ☐ Scrap yarn (to use as st holders)
- ☐ Split ring marker
- ☐ 9/16" (14 mm) Buttons - 3
- ☐ Yarn needle

SIZE INFORMATION

Finished Chest Measurement:
21{23½-25}" / 53.5{59.5-63.5} cm

Size Note: For ease in following the pattern, we have printed the instructions for each size in a different color:

- Size 3-6 months in Blue
- Size 6-9 months in Pink
- Size 9-12 months in Green

GAUGE INFORMATION

In Stockinette Stitch,
16 sts and 20 rows = 4" (10 cm)

TECHNIQUES USED

- YO ***(Photo G, page 5)***
- K2 tog ***(Photo K, page 5)***
- SSK ***(Photos L & M, page 6)***
- Knit Increase ***(Figs. 3a & b, page 32)***

BODY

Neckband

Cast on 48{52-56} sts.

Rows 1 and 2: Knit across.

Row 3 (Right side - Buttonhole row): Knit across to last 4 sts, [K2 tog, YO (buttonhole made)], K2.

Row 4: K4, place marker, knit increase across to last 4 sts, place marker, K4: 88{96-104} sts.

Yoke

Rows 1 and 2: Knit across.

Size 3-6 months ONLY

Row 3: K4, slip marker, ★ (K2, knit increase) twice, K3, knit increase; repeat from ★ to marker, slip marker, K4: 112 sts.

Size 6-9 months ONLY

Row 3: K4, slip marker, K1, knit increase, (K2, knit increase) 28 times, K1, knit increase, slip marker, K4: 126 sts.

Size 9-12 months ONLY

Row 3: K4, slip marker, (K2, knit increase) 32 times, slip marker, K4: 136 sts.

All Sizes

Row 4: Knit across, slipping markers.

Row 5: K4, slip marker, (K2 tog, YO) to marker, slip marker, K4.

Rows 6-8: K4, slip marker, purl to marker, slip marker, K4.

Row 9 (Buttonhole row)**:** Knit across to second marker, slip marker, [K2 tog, YO (buttonhole made)], K2.

Row 10: K4, slip marker, purl to marker, slip marker, K4.

Size 3-6 months ONLY

Row 11: K4, slip marker, ★ (K3, knit increase) twice, K4, knit increase; repeat from ★ to marker, slip marker, K4: 136 sts.

Size 6-9 months ONLY

Row 11: K4, slip marker, K2, knit increase, (K3, knit increase) 28 times, K2, knit increase, slip marker, K4: 156 sts.

Size 9-12 months ONLY

Row 11: K4, slip marker, (K3, knit increase) 32 times, slip marker, K4: 168 sts.

All Sizes

Row 12: Knit across, slipping markers.

Row 13: K4, slip marker, (K2 tog, YO) to marker, slip marker, K4.

Rows 14-16: K4, slip marker, purl to marker, slip marker, K4.

Row 17: Knit across, slipping markers.

Row 18: K4, slip marker, purl to marker, slip marker, K4.

Row 19 (Buttonhole row)**:** Knit across to second marker, slip marker, [K2 tog, YO (buttonhole made)], K2.

Row 20: Knit across, slipping markers.

Row 21: K4, slip marker, (K2 tog, YO) to marker, slip marker, K4.

Rows 22-24: K4, slip marker, purl to marker, slip marker, K4.

Sizes 6-9 months and 9-12 months ONLY

Row 25: Knit across, slipping markers.

Row 26: K4, slip marker, purl to marker, slip marker, K4.

Size 9-12 months ONLY

Rows 27 and 28: Repeat Rows 25 and 26.

All Sizes

DIVIDE FOR LOWER BODY & SLEEVES

Row 1: K4, slip marker, knit 16{19-21} sts for left front, slip next 30{35-38} sts onto st holder for sleeve, **turn**; add on 4 sts for underarm ***(Figs. 8a & b, page 33)***, **turn**; knit 36{40-42} sts for back, slip next 30{35-38} sts onto st holder for sleeve, **turn**; add on 4 sts for underarm, **turn**; knit 20{23-25} sts for right front, slipping marker: 84{94-100} sts.

Row 2: K4, slip marker, purl to marker, slip marker, K4.

Row 3: Knit across, slipping markers.

Repeat Rows 2 and 3 until cardigan measures approximately 4¼{5¼-6¼}" / 11{13.5-16} cm from underarm or until ¾" (2 cm) less than desired finished length, ending by working a **right** side row and removing markers on last row.

Last 6 Rows: Knit across.

Bind off all sts in **knit**.

Sleeve

With **right** side facing and using double-pointed needles, pick up 4{3-4} sts across underarm ***(Figs. 13a & b, page 34)***, knit 30{35-38} sts from st holder: 34{38-42} sts.

Divide the stitches evenly onto four double-pointed needles ***(see Double-Pointed Needles, page 32)***; place a split-ring marker to indicate the beginning of the round ***(see Markers, page 31)***.

Work even in Stockinette Stitch until Sleeve measures approximately 3½{4½-5½}" / 9{11.5-14} cm from underarm.

CUFF

Rnd 1: Purl around.

Rnd 2: Knit around

Rnds 3-5: Repeat Rnds 1 and 2 once; then repeat Rnd 1 once **more**.

Bind off all sts in **knit**.

Repeat for second Sleeve.

FINISHING

Sew buttons opposite buttonholes.

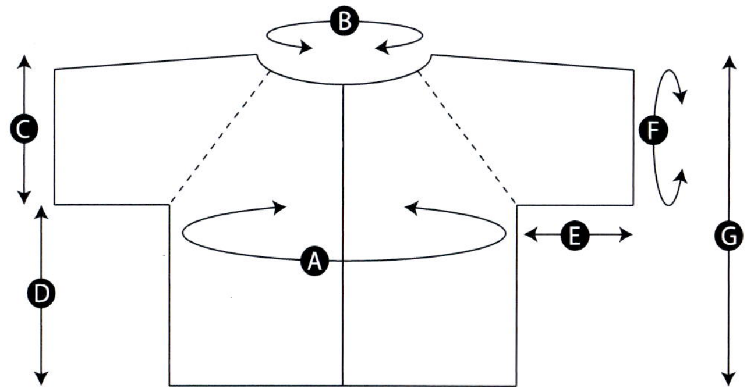

Schematic Label	Description	Imperial Measurement / Metric Measurement
A	Chest Measurement	21{23½-25}" / 53.5{59.5-63.5} cm
B	Neck Circumference	12{13-14}" / 30.5{33-35.5} cm
C	Armhole Depth	4¾{5¼-5½}" / 12{13.5-14} cm
D	Body Length to hem	5{6-7}" / 12.5{15-18} cm
E	Sleeve Length	4¼{5¼-6¼}" / 11{13.5-16} cm
F	Sleeve Circumference	8½{9½-10½}" / 21.5{24-26.5} cm
G	Total Length	9¾{11¼-12½}" / 25{28.5-32} cm

Sampler Cardigan

●●○○ EASY

SHOPPING LIST

Yarn (Medium Weight)

[3½ ounces, 198 yards (100 grams, 181 meters) per skein]:

☐ {8-10-11}{12-13-14} balls

Knitting Needles

29" (73.5 cm) Circular,

☐ Size 8 (5 mm)

or size needed for gauge

Additional Supplies

☐ Split ring marker - 4

☐ Yarn needle

SIZE INFORMATION

Finished Chest Measurement: {38-43-47½}{52½-57-62}"/ {96.5-109-120.5}{133.5-145-157.5} cm

Finished Length: 29" (73.5 cm)

Size Note: For ease in following the pattern, we have printed the instructions for each size in a different color:

- Size Small in Blue
- Size Medium in Pink
- Size Large in Green
- Size 1X in Red
- Size 2X in Purple
- Size 3X in Orange

GAUGE INFORMATION

In Stockinette Stitch,

20 sts and 24 rows = 4" (10 cm)

TECHNIQUES USED

- YO ***(Photo G, page 5)***
- K2 tog ***(Photo K, page 5)***
- SSK ***(Photos L & M, page 6)***
- M1 ***(Figs. 5a & b, page 33)***
- M1P ***(Figs. 6a & b, page 33)***

BACK

Border

Cast on {96-108-120}{132-144-156} sts.

Rows 1-4: (K3, P3) across.

Rows 5-8: (P3, K3) across.

Repeat Rows 1-8 until piece measures approximately 4" (10 cm) from cast on edge, ending by working Row 4 or Row 8 and increasing one st on last row: {97-109-121}{133-145-157} sts.

BORDER

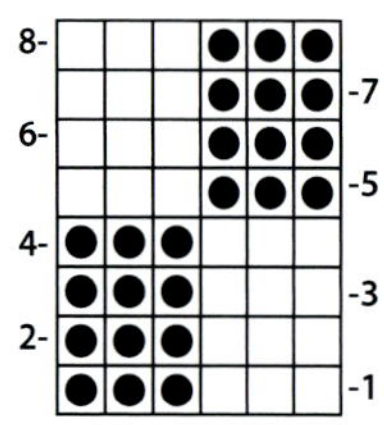

KEY

☐ knit on RS; purl on WS

● knit on WS; purl on RS

Repeat Rows 1-8 for pattern

Follow chart from right to left on RS rows; follow chart from left to right on WS rows.

First Garter Ridge

Rows 1-4: Knit across.

Beginning with a **knit** row, work in Stockinette Stitch until piece measures approximately 13" (33 cm) from cast on edge, ending by working a **purl** row.

Second Garter Ridge

Rows 1-4: Knit across.

First Lace Section

Row 1 (Right side)**:** P1, ★ P2, K2 tog, K1, (YO, K1) twice, SSK, P3; repeat from ★ across.

Row 2: (K3, P7, K2) across to last st, K1.

Row 3: P1, ★ P1, K2 tog, K1, YO, K3, YO, K1, SSK, P2; repeat from ★ across.

Row 4: (K2, P9, K1) across to last st, K1.

Row 5: P1, ★ K2 tog, K1, YO, K5, YO K1, SSK, P1; repeat from ★ across.

Row 6: (K1, P 11) across to last st, K1.

Row 7: P1, (K 11, P1) across.

Row 8: (P3, K7, P2) across to last st, P1.

Row 9: K1, ★ YO, K1, SSK, P5, K2 tog, K1, YO, K1; repeat from ★ across.

Row 10: (P4, K5, P3) across to last st, P1.

Row 11: K1, ★ K1, YO, K1, SSK, P3, K2 tog, K1, YO, K2; repeat from ★ across.

Row 12: (P5, K3, P4) across to last st, P1.

Row 13: K1, ★ K2, YO, K1, SSK, P1, K2 tog, K1, YO, K3; repeat from ★ across.

Row 14: (P6, K1, P5) across to last st, P1.

Row 15: K1, (K5, P1, K6) across.

Row 16: (K4, P5, K3) across to last st, K1.

Repeat Rows 1-16 until piece measures approximately 23" (58.5 cm) from cast on edge, ending by working a **wrong** side row.

Third Garter Ridge

Rows 1-4: Knit across.

Second Lace Section

Row 1: K1, ★ YO, SSK, K1, K2 tog, YO, K1; repeat from ★ across.

Row 2: Purl across.

Repeat Rows 1 and 2 until piece measures approximately 29" (73.5 cm) from cast on edge, ending by working a **purl** row.

Bind off all sts in **knit**.

SECOND LACE SECTION

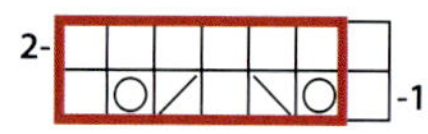

KEY

knit on RS; purl on WS

K2 tog

SSK

YO

pattern repeat

Repeat Rows 1and 2 for pattern

Follow chart from right to left on RS rows; follow chart from left to right on WS rows.

FIRST LACE SECTION
BACK - ALL SIZES
LEFT FRONT - SIZES MEDIUM, 1X AND 3X
RIGHT FRONT - SIZES MEDIUM, 1X AND 3X

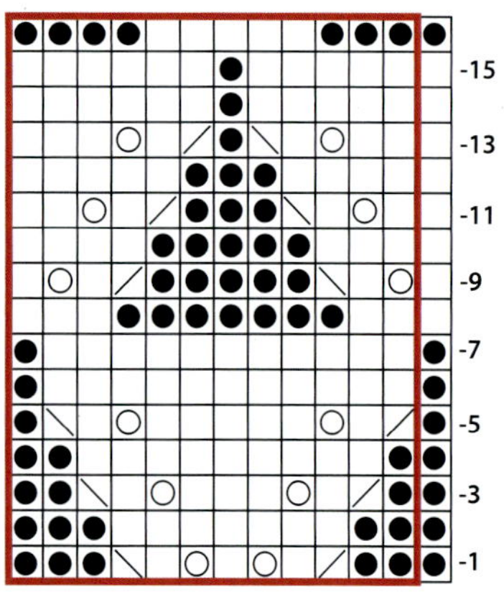

KEY

knit on RS; purl on WS

knit on WS; purl on RS

K2 tog

SSK

YO

pattern repeat

Repeat Rows 1-16 for pattern

Follow chart from right to left on RS rows; follow chart from left to right on WS rows.

LEFT FRONT

Border

Cast on {30-36-42}{48-54-60} sts.

Work same as Back: {31-37-43}{49-55-61} sts.

Sizes Medium, 1X, and 3X ONLY

Complete same as Back, beginning at First Garter Ridge.

Sizes Small, Large, and 2X ONLY
Work same as Back to First Lace Section.

First Lace Section

Row 1: K1, YO, K1, SSK, P3, ★ P2, K2 tog, K1, (YO, K1) twice, SSK, P3; repeat from ★ across.

Row 2: (K3, P7, K2) across to last 7 sts, K3, P4.

Row 3: K2, YO, K1, SSK, P2, ★ P1, K2 tog, K1, YO, K3, YO, K1, SSK, P2; repeat from ★ across.

Row 4: (K2, P9, K1) across to last 7 sts, K2, P5.

Row 5: K3, YO, K1, SSK, P1, ★ K2 tog, K1, YO, K5, YO, K1, SSK, P1; repeat from ★ across.

Row 6: (K1, P 11) across to last 7 sts, K1, P6.

Row 7: K6, P1, (K 11, P1) across.

Row 8: (P3, K7, P2) across to last 7 sts, P3, K4.

Row 9: P3, K2 tog, K1, YO, K1, ★ YO, K1, SSK, P5, K2 tog, K1, YO, K1; repeat from ★ across.

Row 10: (P4, K5, P3) across to last 7 sts, P4, K3.

Row 11: P2, K2 tog, K1, YO, K2, ★ K1, YO, K1, SSK, P3, K2 tog, K1, YO, K2; repeat from ★ across.

Row 12: (P5, K3, P4) across to last 7 sts, P5, K2.

Row 13: P1, K2 tog, K1, YO, K3, ★ K2, YO, K1, SSK, P1, K2 tog, K1, YO, K3; repeat from ★ across.

Row 14: (P6, K1, P5) across to last 7 sts, P6, K1.

Row 15: P1, K6, (K5, P1, K6) across.

Row 16: (K4, P5, K3) across to last 7 sts, K4, P3.

Repeat Rows 1-16 until piece measures approximately 23" (58.5 cm) from cast on edge, ending by working a **wrong** side row.

Complete same as Back, beginning with Third Garter Ridge.

FIRST LACE SECTION
LEFT FRONT - SIZES SMALL, LARGE, AND 2X

KEY
☐ knit on RS; purl on WS
● knit on WS; purl on RS
⧄ K2 tog
⧅ SSK
○ YO
▯ pattern repeat

Repeat Rows 1-16 for pattern

Follow chart from right to left on RS rows; follow chart from left to right on WS rows.

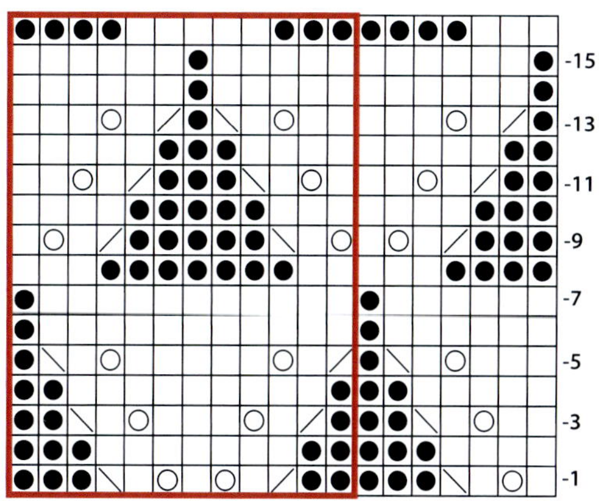

RIGHT FRONT

Border

Cast on {30-36-42}{48-54-60} sts.

Work same as Back: {31-37-43}{49-55-61} sts.

Sizes Medium, 1X, and 3X ONLY

Complete same as Back, beginning at First Garter Ridge.

Sizes Small, Large, and 2X ONLY

Work same as Back to First Lace Section.

First Lace Section

Row 1 (Right side)**:** P3, K2 tog, K1, YO, K1, ★ YO, K1, SSK, P5, K2 tog, K1, YO, K1; repeat from ★ across.

Row 2: (P4, K5, P3) across to last 7 sts, P4, K3.

Row 3: P2, K2 tog, K1, YO, K2, ★ K1, YO, K1, SSK, P3, K2 tog, K1, YO, K2; repeat from ★ across.

FIRST LACE SECTION
RIGHT FRONT - SIZES SMALL, LARGE, AND 2X

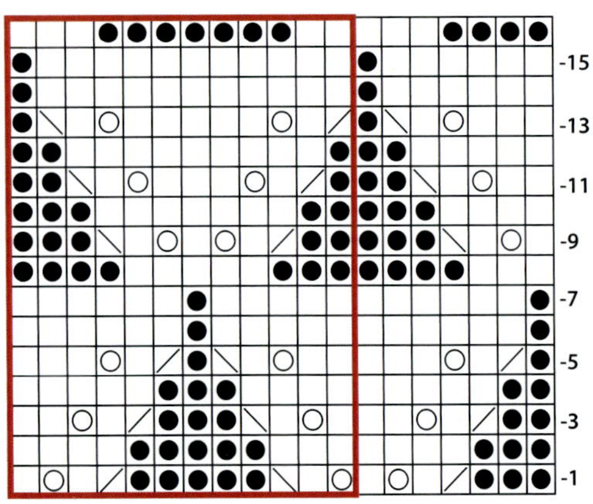

KEY

☐ knit on RS; purl on WS

K2 tog

SSK

YO

pattern repeat

Repeat Rows 1 and 2 for pattern

Follow chart from right to left on RS rows; follow chart from left to right on WS rows.

Row 4: (P5, K3, P4) across to last 7 sts, P5, K2.

Row 5: P1, K2 tog, K1, YO, K3, ★ K2, YO, K1, SSK, P1, K2 tog, K1, YO, K3; repeat from ★ across.

Row 6: (P6, K1, P5) across to last 7 sts, P6, K1.

Row 7: P1, K6, (K5, P1, K6) across.

Row 8: (K4, P5, K3) across to last 7 sts, K4, P3.

Row 9: K1, YO, K1, SSK, P3, ★ P2, K2 tog, K1, (YO, K1) twice, SSK, P3; repeat from ★ across.

Row 10: (K3, P7, K2) across to last 7 sts, K3, P4.

Row 11: K2, YO, K1, SSK, P2, ★ P1, K2 tog, K1, YO, K3, YO, K1, SSK, P2; repeat from ★ across.

Row 12: (K2, P9, K1) across to last 7 sts, K2, P5.

Row 13: K3, YO, K1, SSK, P1, ★ K2 tog, K1, YO, K5, YO, K1, SSK, P1; repeat from ★ across.

Row 14: (K1, P 11) across to last 7 sts, K1, P6.

Row 15: K6, P1, (K 11, P1) across.

Row 16: (P3, K7, P2) across to last 7 sts, P3, K4.

Repeat Rows 1-16 until piece measures approximately 23" (58.5 cm) from cast on edge, ending by working a **wrong** side row.

Complete same as Back, beginning with Third Garter Ridge.

SLEEVE (Make 2)

Cast on 42 sts.

Rows 1 and 2: (K3, P3) across.

Sizes Small and Medium ONLY

Rows 3 and 4: Repeat Rows 1 and 2.

Row 5 (Increase row)**:** K1, M1P, P2, (K3, P3) across to last 3 sts, K2, M1, P1: 44 sts.

Rows 6-8: K1, (P3, K3) across to last st, P1.

Row 9 (Increase row)**:** P1, M1P, (K3, P3) across to last st, M1, K1: 46 sts.

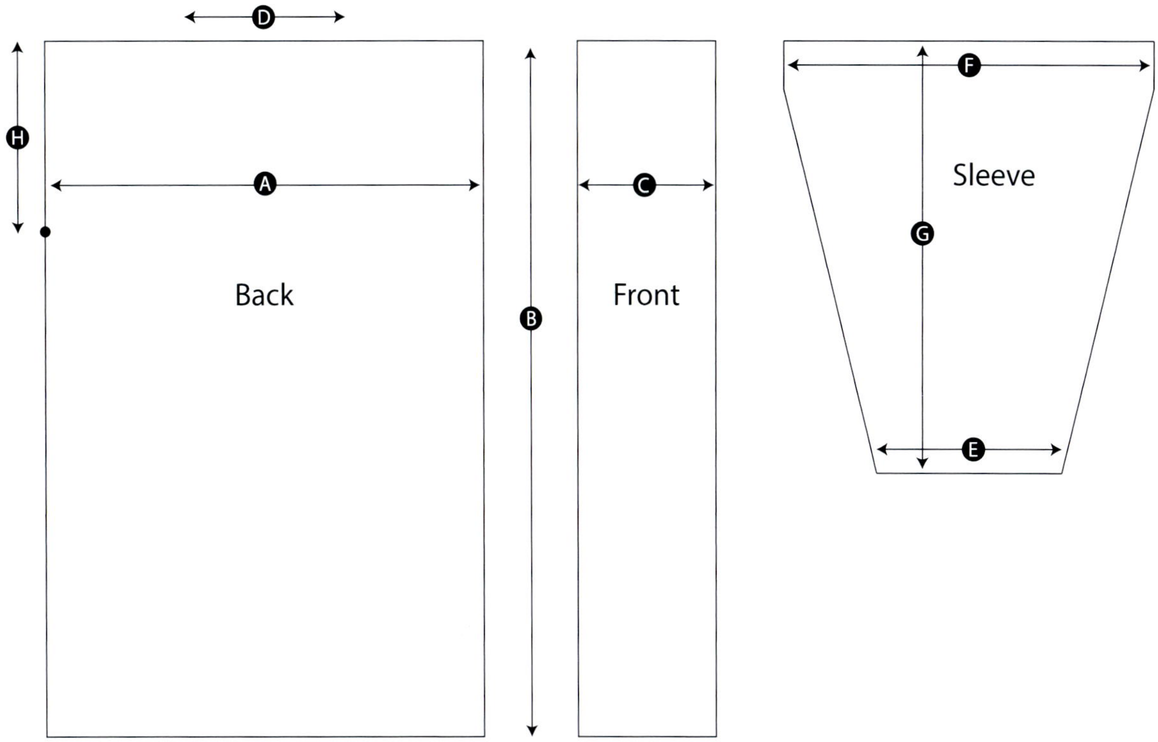

Rows 10-13: Maintaining pattern, continue to increase one st at each edge in same manner, every 4 rows once **more**: 48 sts.

Rows 14-16: Work across in established pattern.

Sizes Large, 1X, 2X and 3X ONLY

Row 3 (Increase row)**:** K1, M1, K2, (P3, K3) across to last 3 sts, P2, M1P, P1: 44 sts.

Row 4: P1, (K3, P3) across to last st, K1.

Row 5 (Increase row)**:** K1, M1, (P3, K3) across to last st, M1P, P1: 46 sts.

Row 6: K2, (P3, K3) across to last 2 sts, P2.

Schematic Label	Description	Imperial Measurement / Metric Measurement
A	Width across Back	{19-21½-23¾}{26¼-28½-31}" / {48.5-54.5-60.5}{66.5-72.5-78.5} cm
B	Total Length	29" / 73.5 cm
C	Width across Right/Left Front	{6¼-7½-8½}{9¾-11-12¼}" / {16-19-21.5}{25-28-31} cm
D	Neck Width	{6½-6½-6¾}{6¾-6½-6½}" / {16.5-16.5-17}{17-16.5-16.5} cm
E	Sleeve Width at Cuff	8½" / 21.5 cm
F	Sleeve Width at Upper Arm	{16-16-17¼}{17¼-18-18}" / {40.5-40.5-44}{44-45.5-45.5} cm
G	Sleeve Length	{19-18¼-17}{15¾-15-14}" / {48.5-46.5-43}{40-38-35.5} cm
H	Armhole Depth	{8-8-8½}{8½-9-9}" / {20.5-20.5-21.5}{21.5-23-23} cm

Size Large ONLY

Rows 7 and 8: Repeat Row 6 twice.

Row 9 (Increase row)**:** P1, M1P, P1, (K3, P3) across to last 2 sts, K1, M1, K1: 48 sts.

Rows 10-16: Maintaining pattern, continue to increase one st in same manner at each edge, every 4 rows once **more**: 50 sts.

Size 1X ONLY

Rows 7-14: Maintaining pattern, continue to increase one st in same manner at each edge, every other row, 4 times **more**: 54 sts.

Rows 15 and 16: Work across in established pattern.

Sizes 2X and 3X ONLY

Rows 7-16: Maintaining pattern, continue to increase one st in same manner at each edge, every other row, 5 times **more**: 56 sts.

All Sizes

Beginning with a **knit** row and working in Stockinette Stitch, continue to increase one st at each edge in same manner, every {4-4-4}{4-2-2} rows, {5-8-18}{16-5-8} times **more**: {58-64-86}{86-66-72} sts.

Sizes Small, Medium, 2X, and 3X ONLY

Continue working in Stockinette Stitch, increasing every {6-6}{4-4} rows, {11-8}{12-9} times: {80-80}{90-90} sts.

All Sizes

Work even until Sleeve measures approximately {19-18¼-17}{15¾-15-14}"/{48.5-46.5-43}{40-38-35.5} cm from cast on edge, ending by working a **purl** row.

Bind off all sts in **knit**.

FINISHING

Sew shoulder seams.

FRONT BAND

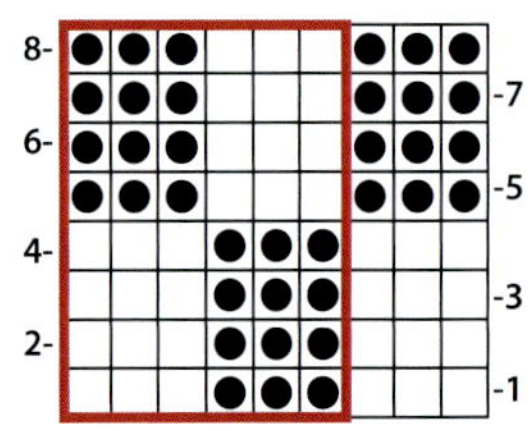

KEY

☐ knit on RS; purl on WS

● knit on WS; purl on RS

▯ pattern repeat

Repeat Rows 1-8 for pattern

Follow chart from right to left on RS rows; follow chart from left to right on WS rows.

Neck & Front Band

With **right** side facing and beginning at lower Right Front, pick up 363 sts evenly spaced along Right Front, Back neck, and Left Front ***(Figs. 13a & b, page 34)***.

Row 1 (WS)**:** K3, (P3, K3) across.

Row 2: P3, (K3, P3) across.

Row 3: K3, (P3, K3) across.

Rows 4 and 5: P3, (K3, P3) across.

Rows 6-8: Repeat Rows 1-3.

Repeat Rows 1-8 until Band measures 8" (20.5 cm), ending by working Row 4 or Row 8.

Bind off all sts in pattern.

Place a marker on each side of Front and Back {8-8-8½}{8½-9-9}"/{20.5-20.5-21.5}{21.5-23-23} cm down from shoulder seam.

Sew Sleeves to Body between markers.

Weave underarm and side in one continuous seam ***(Fig. 16, page 35)***.

Hoodie

●●○○ **EASY**

SHOPPING LIST

Yarn (Bulky Weight) BULKY 5

[5 ounces, 132 yards
(141 grams, 121 meters) per skein]:

☐ {6-7-7}{8-8-9} skeins

Knitting Needles

29" (73.5 cm) Circular,

☐ Size 10½ (6.5 mm)

or size needed for gauge

16" (40.5 cm) Circular,

☐ Size 10½ (6.5 mm)

Double-pointed - 2,

☐ Size 10½ (6.5 mm)

Additional Supplies

☐ Stitch markers - 2

☐ Yarn needle

SIZE INFORMATION

Finished Chest Measurement:

{36¼-40-43¾}{48½-52¼-56)"/
{92-101.5-111}{123-133-142} cm

Finished Length:

{26-26-26½}{26½-27-27}"/
{66-66-67.5}{67.5-68.5-68.5} cm

Size Note: For ease in following the pattern, we have printed the instructions for each size in a different color:

- Size Small in Blue
- Size Medium in Pink
- Size Large in Green
- Size 1X in Red
- Size 2X in Purple
- Size 3X in Orange

GAUGE INFORMATION

In Stockinette Stitch,
13 sts and 19 rows = 4" (10 cm)

TECHNIQUES USED

- YO *(Photo G, page 5)*
- K2 tog *(Photo K, page 5)*
- SSK *(Photos L & M, page 6)*
- S2KP2 *(Photos N thru P, page 6)*
- M1 *(Figs. 5a & b, page 33)*
- P2 tog *(Fig. 10, page 34)*
- SSP *(Fig. 12, page 34)*

FRONT

Ribbing

Cast on {60-66-72}{80-86-92} sts.

Work in K1, P1 ribbing for 2" (5 cm), increasing one st on last row: {61-67-73}{81-87-93} sts.

Body

Beginning with a **knit** row, work in Stockinette Stitch until piece measures approximately 16½" (42 cm) from cast on edge, ending by working a **purl** row.

ARMHOLE SHAPING

Note: Maintain established pattern throughout.

Rows 1 and 2: Bind off {4-4-6}{6-8-8} sts, work across: {53-59-61}{69-71-77} sts.

Work even until Front measures approximately {22-22-22½}{22½-23-23}"/{56-56-57}{57-58.5-58.5} cm from cast on edge, ending by working a **purl** row.

NECK SHAPING

Note: Both sides of Neck are worked at the same time, using separate yarn for **each** side.

Row 1: Knit {20-23-24}{28-29-32} sts; with second ball, bind off next 13 sts, knit across: {20-23-24}{28-29-32} sts **each** side.

Rows 2-5: Work across; with second yarn, bind off 2 sts, work across: {16-19-20}{24-25-28} sts **each** side.

Row 6: Work across to within 2 sts of Neck edge, SSP; with second yarn, P2 tog, purl across: {15-18-19}{23-24-27} sts **each** side.

Work even until Front measures approximately {25-25-25½}{25½-26-26}"/{63.5-63.5-65}{65-66-66} cm from cast on edge, ending by working a **purl** row.

SHOULDER SHAPING

Rows 1 and 2: Bind off {8-9-10}{12-12-14} sts, work across; with second yarn, work across: {7-9-9}{11-12-13} sts **each** side.

Row 3: Bind off sts to Neck edge; with second yarn, knit across.

Row 4: Bind off remaining sts.

BACK

Work same as Front until Back measures approximately {9¼-9¼-9¾}{9¾-10¼-10¼}"/{23.5-23.5-25}{25-26-26} cm from cast on edge, ending by working a **purl** row : {61-67-73}{81-87-93} sts.

Lace Motif

Note: Begin working Lace Motif over center **35 sts** and **AT THE SAME TIME**, when Back measures same as Front to Armhole Shaping, work Armhole Shaping same as Front.

Row 1: Knit {13-16-19}{23-26-29} sts, place marker *(see Markers, page 31)*, K4, YO, SSK, K 23, K2 tog, YO, K4, place marker, knit across.

Row 2 AND ALL WRONG SIDE ROWS: Purl across slipping markers.

Row 3: Knit to marker, slip marker, (K5, YO, SSK) twice, K7, (K2 tog, YO, K5) twice, slip marker, knit across.

Row 5: Knit to marker, slip marker, K6, YO, SSK, K2, K2 tog, YO, K1, YO, SSK, K5, K2 tog, YO, K1, YO, SSK, K2, K2 tog, YO, K6, slip marker, knit across.

Row 7: Knit to marker, slip marker, K7, YO, SSK, K1, K2 tog, YO, K2, YO, SSK, K3, K2 tog, YO, K2, YO, SSK, K1, K2 tog, YO, K7, slip marker, knit across.

Row 9: Knit to marker, slip marker, K8, YO, SSK, K2 tog, YO, K3, YO, SSK, K1, K2 tog, YO K3, YO, SSK, K2 tog, YO, K8, slip marker, knit across.

Rows 11 and 13: Knit to marker, slip marker, K 10, K2 tog, YO, K4, YO, S2KP2, YO, K4, YO, SSK, K 10, slip marker, knit across.

Row 15: Knit to marker, slip marker, K8, K2 tog, YO, K2, YO, SSK, K2, YO, S2KP2, YO, K2, K2 tog, YO, K2, YO, SSK, K8, slip marker, knit across.

Row 17: Knit to marker, slip marker, K7, K2 tog, YO, K1, (YO, SSK, K1) twice, YO, S2KP2, YO, K1, (K2 tog, YO, K1) twice, YO, SSK, K7, slip marker, knit across.

Row 19: Knit to marker, slip marker, K6, K2 tog, YO, K3, YO, SSK, K1, YO, SSK, YO, S2KP2, YO, K2 tog, YO, K1, K2 tog, YO, K3, YO, SSK, K6, slip marker, knit across.

Row 21: Knit to marker, slip marker, K1, K2 tog, YO, K2, K2 tog, YO, K5, (YO, SSK, K1) twice, K2 tog, YO, K1, K2 tog, YO, K5, YO, SSK, K2, YO, SSK, K1, slip marker, knit across.

Row 23: Knit to marker, slip marker, K1, YO, S2KP2, YO, K2 tog, YO, K7, YO, SSK, K5, K2 tog, YO, K7, YO, SSK, YO, S2KP2, YO, K1, slip marker, knit across.

Row 25: Knit to marker, slip marker, YO, SSK, K1, K2 tog, YO, K9, K2 tog, YO, K3, YO, SSK, K9, YO, SSK, K1, K2 tog, YO, slip marker, knit across.

LACE MOTIF

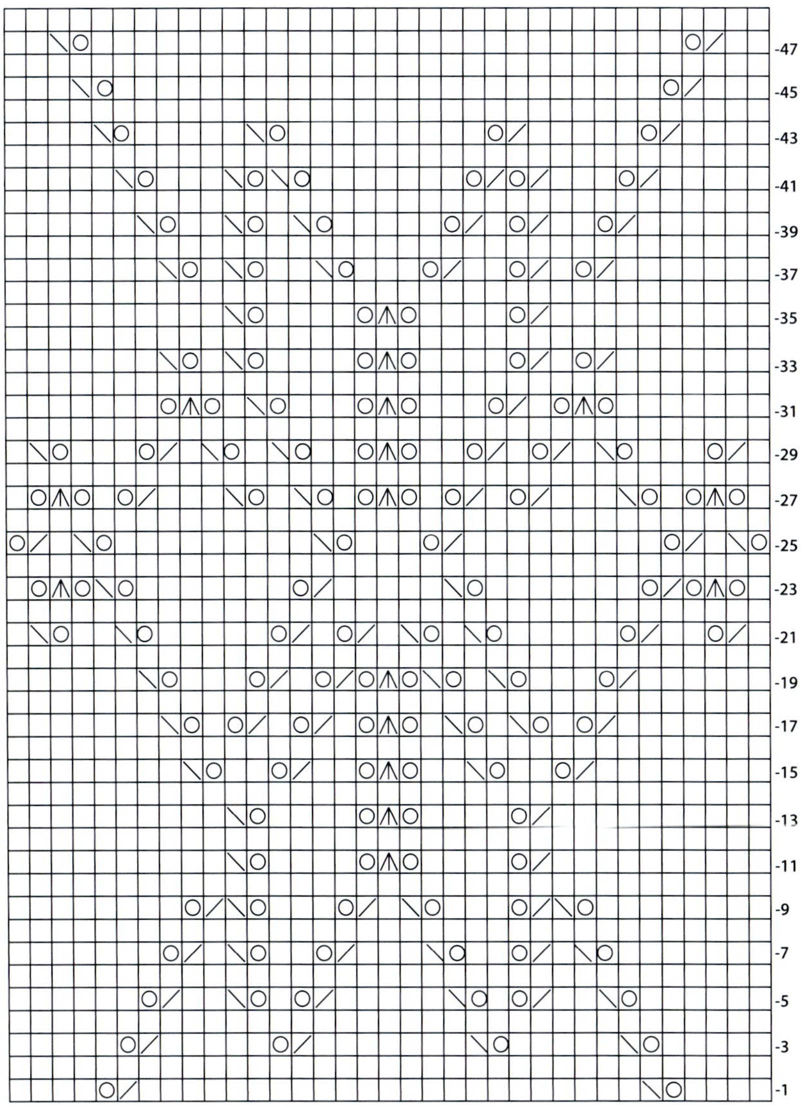

KEY

knit on RS; purl on WS

K2 tog

SSK

YO

S2KP2

Work Rows 1-48 for pattern

Follow chart from right to left on RS rows; follow chart from left to right on WS rows.

Row 27: Knit to marker, slip marker, K1, YO, S2KP2, YO, K1, YO, SSK, K3, (K2 tog, YO, K1) twice, YO, S2KP2, YO, (K1, YO, SSK) twice, K3, K2 tog, YO, K1, YO, S2KP2, YO, K1, slip marker, knit across.

Row 29: Knit to marker, slip marker, K1, K2 tog, YO, K3, YO, SSK, (K1, K2 tog, YO) twice, K2, YO, S2KP2, YO, K2, (YO, SSK, K1) twice, K2 tog, YO, K3, YO, SSK, K1, slip marker, knit across.

Row 31: Knit to marker, slip marker, K7, YO, S2KP2, YO, K1, K2 tog, YO, K3, YO, S2KP2, YO, K3, YO, SSK, K1, YO, S2KP2, YO, K7, slip marker, knit across.

Row 33: Knit to marker, slip marker, K7, K2 tog, YO, K1, K2 tog, YO, K4, YO, S2KP2, YO, K4, YO, SSK, K1, YO, SSK, K7, slip marker, knit across.

Row 35: Knit to marker, slip marker, K 10, K2 tog, YO, K4, YO, S2KP2, YO, K4, YO, SSK, K 10, slip marker, knit across.

Row 37: Knit to marker, slip marker, K7, K2 tog, YO, K1, K2 tog, YO, K2, K2 tog, YO, K3, YO, SSK, K2, YO, SSK, K1, YO, SSK, K7, slip marker, knit across.

Row 39: Knit to marker, slip marker, K6, K2 tog, YO, K2, K2 tog, YO, K1, K2 tog, YO, K5, YO, SSK, K1, YO, SSK, K2, YO, SSK, K6, slip marker, knit across.

Row 41: Knit to marker, slip marker, K5, K2 tog, YO, K3, (K2 tog, YO) twice, K7, (YO, SSK) twice, K3, YO, SSK, K5, slip marker, knit across.

Row 43: Knit to marker, slip marker, K4, K2 tog, YO, K5, K2 tog, YO, K9, YO, SSK, K5, YO, SSK, K4, slip marker, knit across.

Row 45: Knit to marker, slip marker, K3, K2 tog, YO, K 25, YO, SSK, K3, slip marker, knit across.

Row 47: Knit to marker, slip marker, K2, K2 tog, YO, K 27, YO, SSK, K2, slip marker, knit across.

Work in Stockinette Stitch until Back measures approximately {25-25-25½}{25½-26-26}"/{63.5-63.5-65}{65-66-66} cm from cast on edge, ending by working a **purl** row: {53-59-61}{69-71-77} sts.

SHOULDER SHAPING

Rows 1 and 2: Bind off {8-9-10}{12-12-14} sts, work across: {37-41-41}{45-47-49} sts.

Rows 3 and 4: Bind off {7-9-9}{11-12-13} sts, work across: 23 sts.

Bind off remaining sts in **knit**.

SLEEVE (Make 2)

Ribbing

Cast on 30 sts.

Work in K1, P1 ribbing for 2" (5 cm).

Body

Beginning with a **knit** row, work in Stockinette Stitch, increasing one st at each edge, every {6-4-4}{4-2-2} rows, {13-1-10}{12-4-5} time(s); then increase every {0-6-6}{6-4-4} rows, {0-12-5}{3-13-12} times ***(see Zeros, page 31)***: {56-56-60}{60-64-64} sts.

Work even until Sleeve measures approximately {20½-20-19½}{18½-18-17½}" / {52-51-49.5}{47-45.5-44.5} cm from cast on edge, ending by working a **purl** row.

Bind off all sts in **knit**.

FINISHING

Sew shoulder seams.

Hood

With **right** side facing, using 16" (40.5 cm) circular needle, and beginning at center front neck, pick up 71 sts evenly spaced around neck edge ***(Figs. 13a & b, page 34)***; do **not** join.

Row 1: (P1, K1) 3 times, purl across to last 6 sts, (K1, P1) 3 times.

Row 2 (RS)**:** (K1, P1) 3 times, knit across to last 6 sts, (P1, K1) 3 times.

Repeat Rows 1 and 2 until Hood measures approximately 1" (2.5 cm), ending by working a **wrong** side row.

Next Row (Increase row)**:** (K1, P1) 3 times, K 29, M1, place marker, K1, place marker, M1, knit across to last 6 sts, (P1, K1) 3 times: 73 sts.

Maintaining pattern, continue to increase one st on each side of center st, every 6 rows, 5 times **more**: 83 sts.

Work even until Hood measures approximately 12½" (32 cm) from cast on edge, ending by working a **wrong** side row and decreasing one st at center of last row: 82 sts.

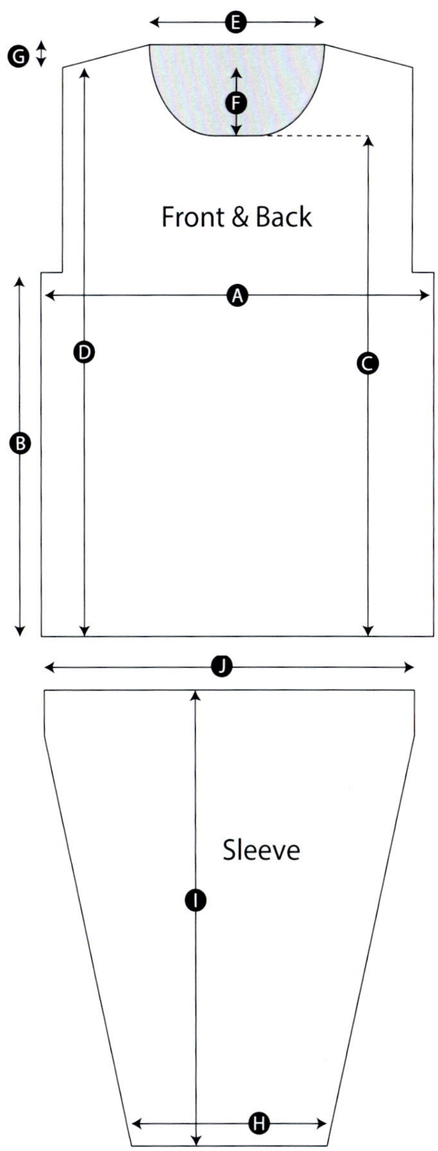

Divide the stitches evenly on two double-pointed needles.

Holding stitches with **right** sides together, work three needle bind off *(Fig. 15, page 35)*.

Front Pocket (Optional)

Cast on 59 sts.

Row 1: (P1, K1) 3 times, purl across to last 6 sts, (K1, P1) 3 times.

Row 2 (RS)**:** (K1, P1) 3 times, knit across to last 6 sts, (P1, K1) 3 times.

Row 3: (P1, K1) 3 times, purl across to last 6 sts, (K1, P1) 3 times.

Row 4 (Decrease row)**:** (K1, P1) 3 times, SSK, knit across to last 8 sts, K2 tog, (P1, K1) 3 times: 57 sts.

Maintaining pattern, continue to decrease one st at each edge, every other row, 5 times **more**; then decrease every 4 rows, 6 times: 35 sts.

Bind off all sts in pattern.

Using photo as a guide, sew the lower and upper edges of pocket to Front, leaving sides open.

Set in sleeves.
Weave underarm and side in one continuous seam *(Fig. 16, page 35)*.

Schematic Label	Description	Imperial Measurement / Metric Measurement
A	Front and Back Width	{18¼-20-21¾}{24¼-26¼-28}" / {46.5-51-55}{61.5-66.5-71} cm
B	Body Length to Underarm	16½" / 42 cm
C	Body Length to Neck Shaping	{22-22-22½}{22½-23-23}" / {56-56-57}{57-58.5-58.5} cm
D	Body Length to Shoulder Shaping	{25-25-25½}{25½-26-26}" / {63.5-63.5-65}{65-66-66} cm
E	Neck Width	7" / 18 cm
F	Front Neck Depth	3" / 7.5 cm
G	Shoulder Shaping	1" / 2.5 cm
H	Sleeve Width at Cuff	9¼" / 23.5 cm
I	Sleeve Length	{20½-20-19½}{18½-18-17½}" / {52-51-49.5}{47-45.5-44.5} cm
J	Sleeve Width at Upper Arm	{17¼-17¼-18½}{18½-19¾-19¾}" / {44-44-47}{47-50-50} cm

Crop Top

●●○○ EASY

SHOPPING LIST

Yarn (Medium Weight) MEDIUM 4

[3½ ounces, 186 yards

(100 grams, 170 meters) per skein]:

- ☐ {7-8}{9-10-11} skeins

Knitting Needles

29" (73.5 cm) Circular,

- ☐ Size 6 (4 mm)

  or size needed for gauge

Additional Supplies

- ☐ Yarn needle

SIZE INFORMATION

Finished Chest Measurement:

{38-44½}{50¾-57¼-63½}"/

{96.5-113}{129-145.5-161.5} cm

Finished Length:

{18-18}{18½-18½-19}"/

{45.5-45.5}{47-47-48.5} cm

Size Note: For ease in following the pattern, we have printed the instructions for each size in a different color:

- Size Small in Blue
- Size Medium in Pink
- Size Large in Green
- Size 1X in Red
- Size 2X in Purple

GAUGE INFORMATION

In pattern,

20 sts and 32 rows = 4" (10 cm)

TECHNIQUES USED

- YO ***(Photo G, page 5)***
- K2 tog ***(Photo K, page 5)***
- SSK ***(Photos L & M, page 6)***
- P2 tog ***(Fig. 10, page 34)***
- SSP ***(Fig. 12, page 34)***

BACK

Lower Band

Cast on {87-102}{116-131-145} sts.

Work in Garter Stitch for 1" (2.5 cm), increasing {10-11}{13-14-16} sts evenly spaced across last row ***(see Increasing Evenly Across A Row, page 32)***: {97-113}{129-145-161} sts.

Body

Row 1 (Right side)**:** P1, ★ P2, SSK, K3, YO, K1, YO, K3, K2 tog, P3; repeat from ★ across.

Row 2 AND ALL WRONG SIDE ROWS: Purl across.

Row 3: P1, ★ P2, SSK, K2, YO, K3, YO, K2, K2 tog, P3; repeat from ★ across.

Row 5: P1, ★ P2, SSK, K1, YO, K5, YO, K1, K2 tog, P3; repeat from ★ across.

Row 7: P1, ★ P2, SSK, YO, K7, YO, K2 tog, P3; repeat from ★ across.

Row 9: K1, ★ YO, K3, K2 tog, P5, SSK, K3, YO, K1; repeat from ★ across.

Row 11: K1, ★ K1, YO, K2, K2 tog, P5, SSK, K2, YO, K2; repeat from ★ across.

Row 13: K1, ★ K2, YO, K1, K2 tog, P5, SSK, K1, YO, K3; repeat from ★ across.

Row 15: K1, ★ K3, YO, K2 tog, P5, SSK, YO, K4; repeat from ★ across.

Row 16: Purl across.

CHART

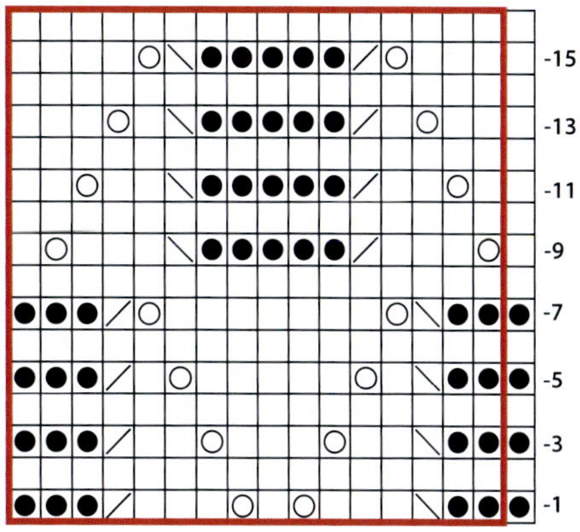

KEY

☐ knit on RS; purl on WS

● purl on RS

⟋ K 2tog

⟍ SSK

○ YO

▯ pattern repeat

Repeat Rows 1-16 for pattern.

Follow chart from right to left on RS rows; follow chart from left to right on WS rows.

Repeat Rows 1-16 for pattern until piece measures approximately 9" (23 cm) from cast on edge, ending by working a **purl** row.

ARMHOLE SHAPING

Note: Maintain established pattern throughout.

Rows 1 and 2: Bind off {8-8}{16-16-24} sts, work across: {81-97}{97-113-113} sts.

Work even until piece measures approximately {15-15}{15½-15½-16}"/{38-38}{39.5-39.5-40.5} cm from cast on edge, ending by working a **wrong** side row.

NECK SHAPING

Note: Both sides of Neck are worked at the same time, using separate yarn for **each** side.

Row 1: Work across first {25-33}{33-41-41} sts; with second yarn, bind off next 31 sts, work across: {25-33}{33-41-41} sts **each** side.

Rows 2 and 3: Work across to Neck edge; with second yarn, bind off 4 sts, work across: {21-29}{29-37-37} sts **each** side.

Rows 4 and 5: Work across to Neck edge; with second yarn, bind off 2 sts, work across: {19-27}{27-35-35} sts **each** side.

Row 6: Purl across to within 2 sts of Neck edge, SSP; with second yarn, P2 tog, purl across: {18-26}{26-34-34} sts **each** side.

Work even until piece measures approximately {17-17}{17½-17½-18}"/{43-43}{44.5-44.5-45.5} cm from cast on edge, ending by working a **wrong** side row.

SHOULDER SHAPING

Rows 1-6: Bind off {5-6}{6-8-8} sts, work across to Neck edge; with second yarn, work across: {3-8}{8-10-10} sts **each** side.

Row 7: Bind off sts to Neck edge; with second yarn, work across.

Bind off remaining sts.

FRONT

Work same as Back.

SLEEVE (Make 2)

Lower Band

Cast on 44 sts.

Work in Garter Stitch for 1" (2.5 cm), increasing 5 sts evenly spaced across last row: 49 sts.

Body

Work in pattern same as Back, increasing one st at **each** edge, every {8-8}{6-6-4} rows, {10-15}{9-17-6} times; then increase every {10-10}{8-8-6} rows, {6-1}{9-1-15} time(s): {81-81}{85-85-91} sts.

Work even until Sleeve measures approximately {20½-19¼}{19¼-17¾-18¼}"/{52-49}{49-45-46.5} cm from cast on edge, ending by working a **purl** row.

Bind off all sts in **knit**.

FINISHING

Sew right shoulder seam.

Neckband

With the **right** side facing, pick up 120 sts evenly spaced along neck edge (***Figs. 13a & b, page 34***).

Work in Garter St for ½" (12 mm).

Next Row: Knit across decreasing 12 sts evenly spaced: 108 sts.

Work even until Neckband measures 1" (2.5 cm).

Bind off all sts loosely in **knit**.

Sew left shoulder seam and end of rows on Neckband.

Set in Sleeves.

Weave underarm and side in one continuous seam ***(Fig. 16, page 35)***, leaving Lower Band free on Front and Back for side vents.

Schematic Label	Description	Imperial Measurement / Metric Measurement
A	Chest Measurement	{38-44½}{50¾-57¼-63½}" / {96.5-113}{129-145.5-161.5} cm
B	Body Length to Underarm	9" / 23 cm
C	Body Length to Neck Shaping	{15-15}{15½-15½-16}" / {38-38}{39.5-39.5-40.5} cm
D	Body Length to Shoulder Shaping	{17-17}{17½-17½-18}" / {43-43}{44.5-44.5-45.5} cm
E	Body Width across Shoulders	{15¾-19}{19-22¼-22¼}" / {40-48.5}{48.5-56.5-56.5} cm
F	Neck Width	9" / 23 cm
G	Neck Depth	2" / 5 cm
H	Shoulder Shaping	¾" / 19 mm
I	Sleeve Width at Cuff	9½" / 24 cm
J	Sleeve Length	{20½-19¼}{19¼-17¾-18¼}" / {52-49}{49-45-46.5} cm
K	Sleeve Width at Upper Arm	{15¾-15¾}{16½-16½-17¾}" / {40-40}{42-42-45} cm

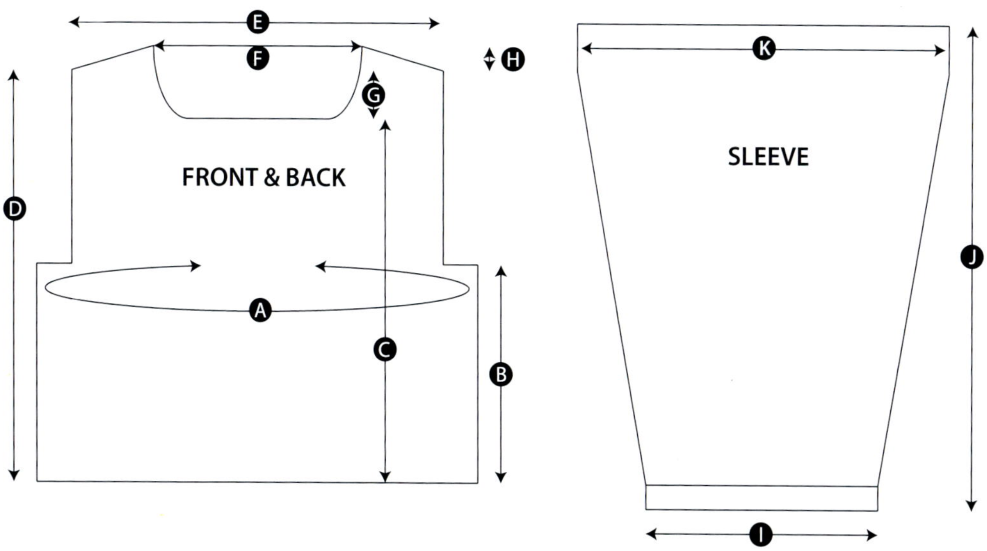

GENERAL INSTRUCTIONS

ABBREVIATIONS

C8B	Cable 8 Back
C8F	Cable 8 Front
CC	Contrasting Color
cm	centimeters
K	knit
M1	make one
MC	Main Color
mm	millimeters
P	purl
PSSO	pass slipped stitch over
P2SSO	pass 2 slipped stitches over
Rnd(s)	Round(s)
RS	right side
S2KP2	slip 2, knit 1, pass 2 slipped stitches over
SSK	slip, slip, knit
SSP	slip, slip, purl
SSSK	slip, slip, slip, knit
st(s)	stitch(es)
tbl	through back loop(s)
tog	together
WS	wrong side
YO	yarn over

SYMBOLS & TERMS

★ — work instructions following ★ as many **more** times as indicated in addition to the first time.

† to † — work all instructions from first † to second † **as many** times as specified.

( ) or [ ] — work enclosed instructions **as many** times as specified by the number immediately following **or** work all enclosed instructions in the stitch or space indicated **or** contains explanatory remarks.

colon (:) — the number(s) given after a colon at the end of a row or round denote(s) the number of stitches and spaces you should have on that row or round.

work even — work without increasing or decreasing in the established pattern.

KNIT TERMINOLOGY		
UNITED STATES		INTERNATIONAL
gauge	=	tension
bind off	=	cast off
yarn over (YO)	=	yarn forward (yfwd) **or** yarn around needle (yrn)

Yarn Weight Symbol & Names	LACE 0	SUPER FINE 1	FINE 2	LIGHT 3	MEDIUM 4	BULKY 5	SUPER BULKY 6	JUMBO 7
Type of Yarns in Category	Fingering, size 10 crochet thread	Sock, Fingering, Baby	Sport, Baby	DK, Light Worsted	Worsted, Afghan, Aran	Chunky, Craft, Rug	Super Bulky, Roving	Jumbo, Roving
Knit Gauge Ranges in Stockinette St to 4" (10 cm)	33-40 sts**	27-32 sts	23-26 sts	21-24 sts	16-20 sts	12-15 sts	7-11 sts	6 sts and fewer
Advised Needle Size Range	000 to 1	1 to 3	3 to 5	5 to 7	7 to 9	9 to11	11 to 17	17 and larger

* GUIDELINES ONLY: The chart above reflects the most commonly used gauges and needle sizes for specific yarn categories.

** Lace weight yarns are usually knitted on larger needles to create lacy openwork patterns. Accordingly, a gauge range is difficult to determine. Always follow the gauge stated in your pattern.

GAUGE

Exact gauge is essential for proper size. Before beginning your project, make a sample swatch in the yarn and needle specified in the individual instructions. After completing the swatch, measure it, counting your stitches and rows carefully. If your swatch is larger or smaller than specified, **make another, changing needle size to get the correct gauge**. Keep trying until you find the size needles that will give you the specified gauge.

MARKERS

As a convenience to you, we have used markers to help distinguish the beginning of a pattern. Place markers as instructed. You may use purchased markers or tie a length of contrasting color yarn around the needle. When you reach a marker on each row or round, slip it from the left needle to the right needle; remove it when no longer needed.

HINTS

As in all pieces, good finishing techniques make a big difference in the quality of the piece. Do **not** tie knots. Always start a new ball at the beginning of a row, leaving ends long enough to weave in later.

ZEROS

To consolidate the length of an involved pattern, Zeros are sometimes used so that all sizes can be combined. For example, increase every sixth row 5{1-0} time(s) means the first size would increase 5 times, the second size would increase once, and the largest size would do nothing.

●○○○ **BASIC**	Projects using basic stitches. May include basic increases and decreases.
●●○○ **EASY**	Projects may include simple stitch patterns, color work, and/or shaping.
●●●○ **INTERMEDIATE**	Projects may include involved stitch patterns, color work, and/or shaping.
●●●● **COMPLEX**	Projects may include complex stitch patterns, color work, and/or shaping using a variety of techniques and stitches simultaneously.

KNITTING NEEDLES																			
U.S.	0	1	2	3	4	5	6	7	8	9	10	$10^1/_2$	11	13	15	17	19	35	50
U.K.	13	12	11	10	9	8	7	6	5	4	3	2	1	00	000	---	---	---	---
Metric - mm	2	2.25	2.75	3.25	3.5	3.75	4	4.5	5	5.5	6	6.5	8	9	10	12.75	15	19	25

CIRCULAR KNITTING
Using Circular Needle

When you knit a tube, as for the body of a pullover, you are going to work around on the outside of the circle, with the **right** side of the knitting facing you.

Using a circular needle, cast on all stitches as instructed. Untwist and straighten the stitches on the needle to be sure that the cast on ridge lays on the inside of the needle and never rolls around the needle.

Hold the needle so that the ball of yarn is attached to the stitch closest to the right hand point. Place a marker on the right hand point to mark the beginning of the round.

To begin working in the round, knit the stitches on the left hand point ***(Fig. 1)***.

Continue working each round as instructed without turning the work; but for the first three rounds or so, check to be sure that the cast on edge has not twisted around the needle. If it has, it is impossible to untwist it. The only way to fix this is to rip it out and return to the cast on row.

Fig. 1

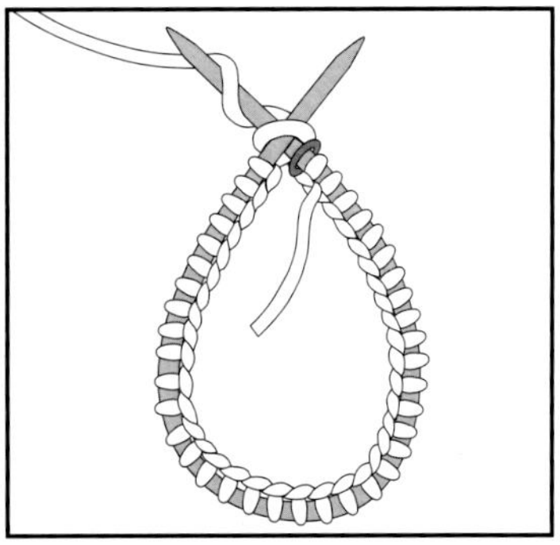

Double Pointed Needles

When working too few stitches to use a circular needle, double pointed needles are required. Divide the stitches between three or four double pointed needles as specified in individual pattern. Being careful not to twist the cast on ridge, form a triangle with the three needles, or a square with the four needles. With the working yarn coming from the stitch on the last needle, work across the stitches on the first needle ***(Fig. 2)***. You will now have an empty needle with which to knit the stitches from the next needle. Work the first stitch of each needle firmly to prevent gaps. Continue working around without turning the work. If there is a yarn over at the end of the needle, take care not to lose it.

Fig. 2

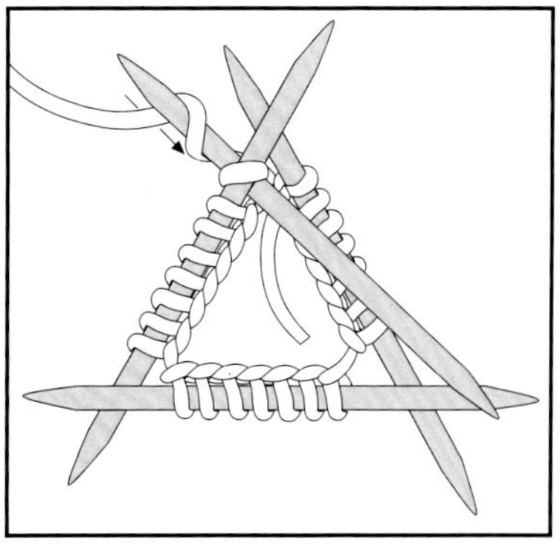

INCREASES
Increasing Evenly Across A Row

Add one to the number of increases required and divide that number into the number of stitches on the needle. Subtract one from the result and the new number is the approximate number of stitches to be worked between each increase. Adjust the number as needed.

Knit Increase

Knit the next stitch but do **not** slip the old stitch off the left needle ***(Fig. 3a)***. Insert the right needle into the **back** loop of the **same** stitch and knit it ***(Fig. 3b)***, then slip the old stitch off the left needle.

Fig. 3a

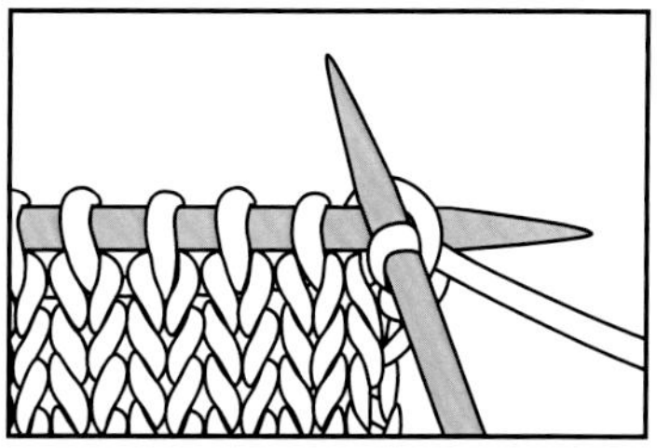

Fig. 3b

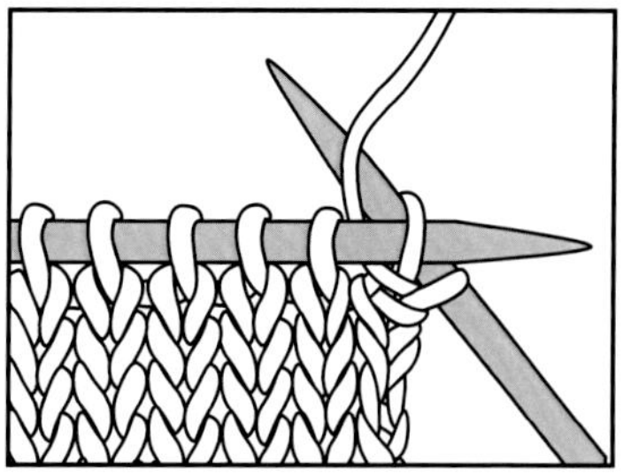

Purl Increase

Purl the next stitch but do **not** slip the old stitch off the left needle. Insert the right needle into the **back** loop of the **same** stitch and purl it ***(Fig. 4)***, then slip the old stitch off the left needle.

Fig. 4

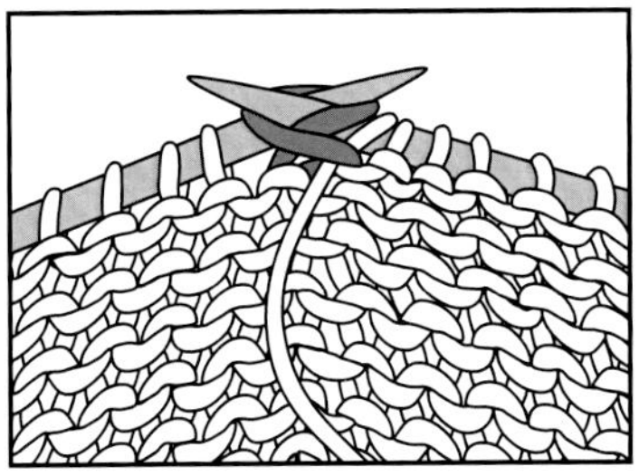

Make One *(abbreviated M1)*

Insert the **left** needle under the horizontal strand between the stitches from the **front** ***(Fig. 5a)***. Then **knit** into the **back** of the strand ***(Fig. 5b)***.

Fig. 5a

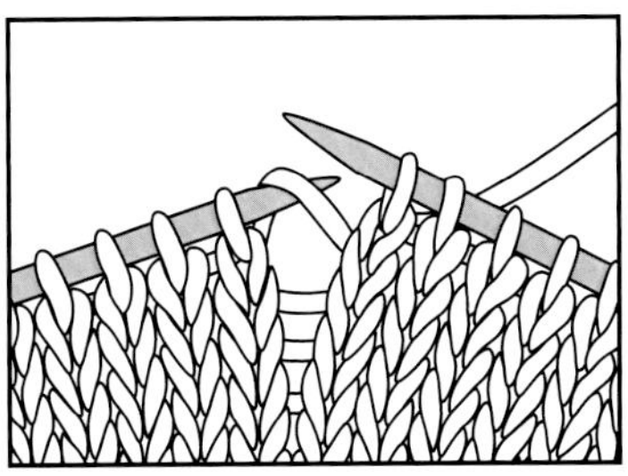

Fig. 5b

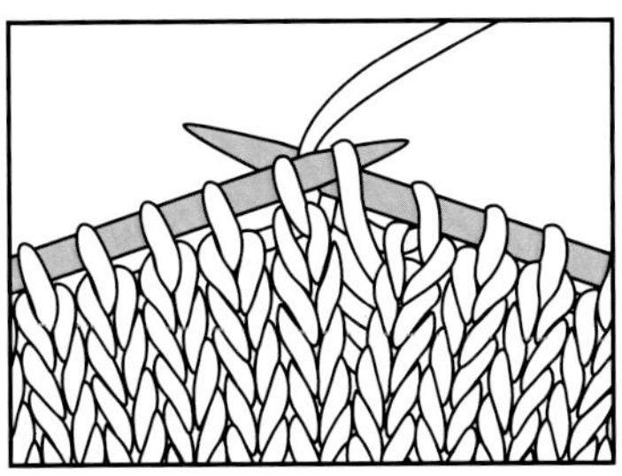

Make One Purl *(abbreviated M1P)*

Insert the **left** needle under the horizontal strand between the stitches from the **back** ***(Fig. 6a)***. Then **purl** into the **front** of the strand ***(Fig. 6b)***.

Fig. 6a

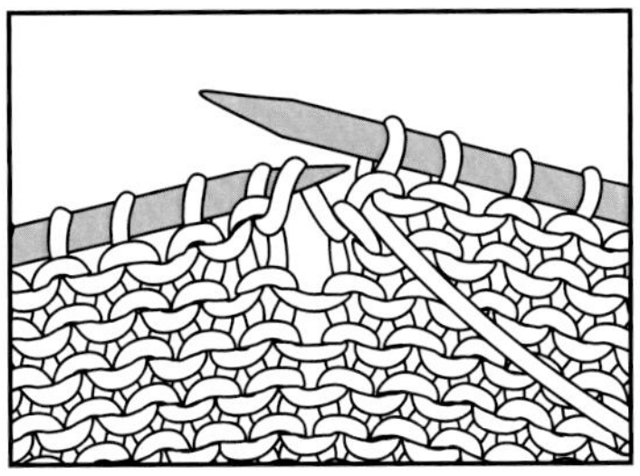

Fig. 6b

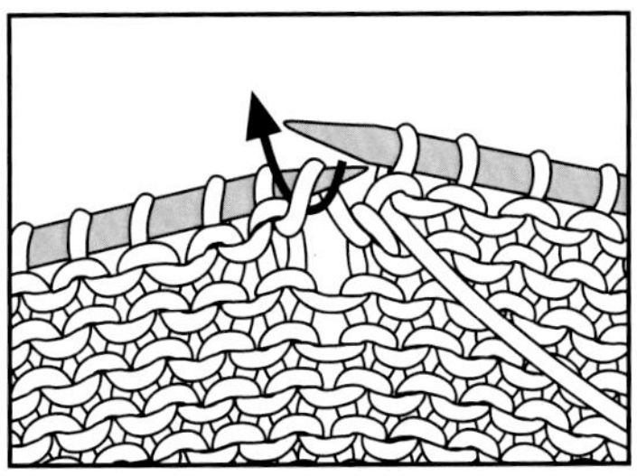

Yarn Over Twice

★ Bring the yarn forward **between** the needles, then back **over** the top of the right hand needle; repeat from ★ once **more**, so that it is now in position to knit the next stitch ***(Fig. 7)***.

Fig. 7

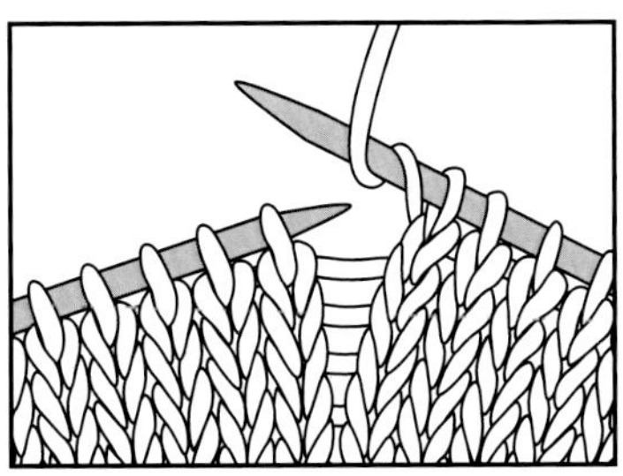

Adding New Stitches

Insert the right needle into the stitch as if to **knit**, yarn over and pull loop through ***(Fig. 8a)***, insert the left needle into the loop just worked from **front** to **back** and slip the loop onto the left needle ***(Fig. 8b)***. Repeat for the required number of stitches.

Fig. 8a

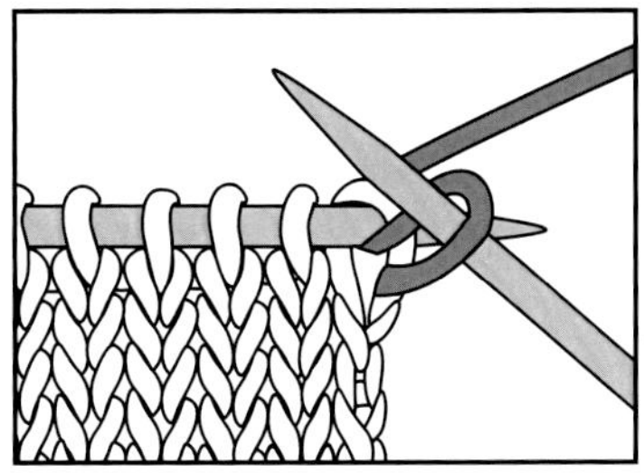

Fig. 8b

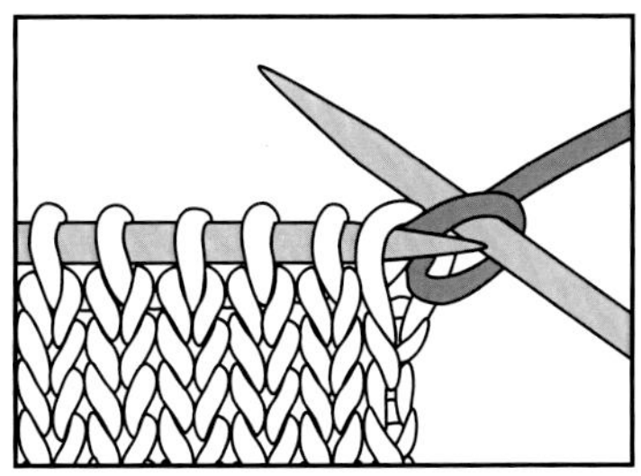

DECREASES

Knit 2 Together Through Back Loop *(abbreviated K2 tog tbl)*

Insert the right needle into the **back** of first two stitches on the left needle from **front** to **back** *(Fig. 9)*, then **knit** them together as if they were one stitch.

Fig. 9

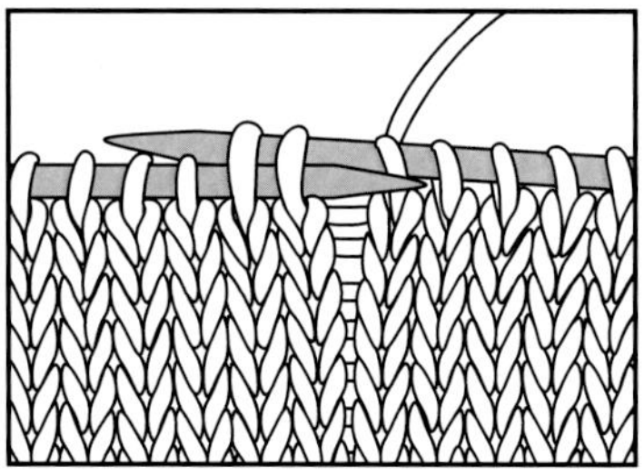

Purl 2 Together *(abbreviated P2 tog)*

Insert the right needle into the **front** of the first two stitches on the left needle as if to **purl** *(Fig. 10)*, then **purl** them together as if they were one stitch.

Fig. 10

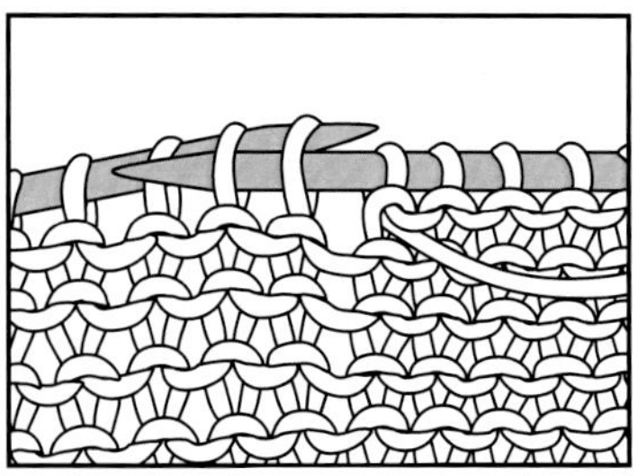

Knit 3 Together *(abbreviated K3 tog)*

Insert the right needle into the **front** of the first three stitches on the left needle as if to **knit** *(Fig. 11)*, then **knit** them together as if they were one stitch.

Fig. 11

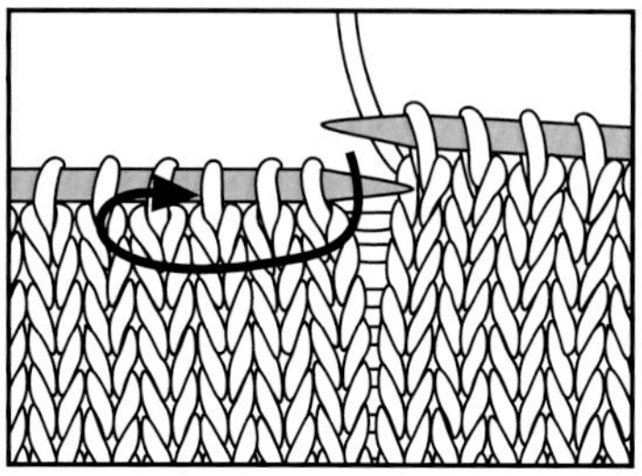

Slip, Slip, Purl *(abbreviated SSP)*

Separately slip two stitches as if to **knit**. Place these two stitches back onto the left needle. Insert the right needle into the **back** of both stitches from **back** to **front** *(Fig. 12)* and **purl** them together as if they were one stitch.

Fig. 12

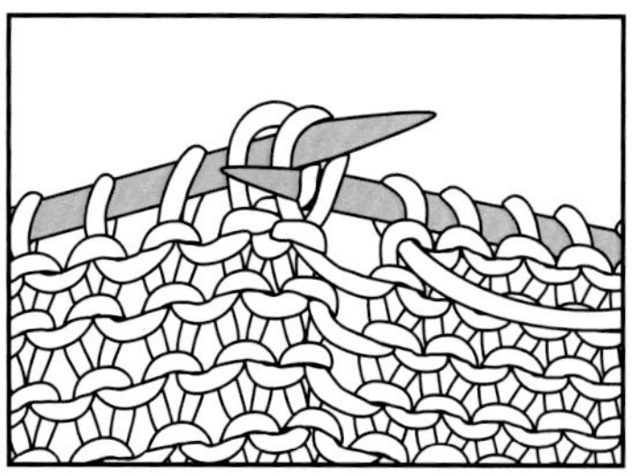

PICKING UP STITCHES

When instructed to pick up stitches, insert the needle from the **front** to the **back** under two strands at the edge of the worked piece *(Figs. 13a & b)*.

Put the yarn around the needle as if to **knit**, then bring the needle with the yarn back through the stitch to the right side, resulting in a stitch on the needle.

Repeat this along the edge, picking up the required number of stitches.

A crochet hook may be helpful to pull yarn through.

Fig. 13a

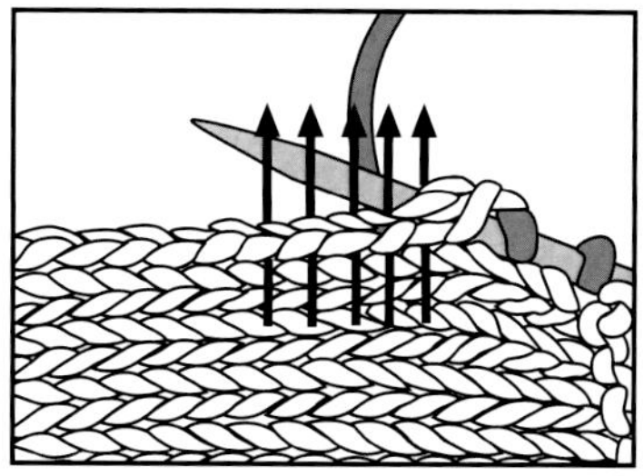

Fig. 13b

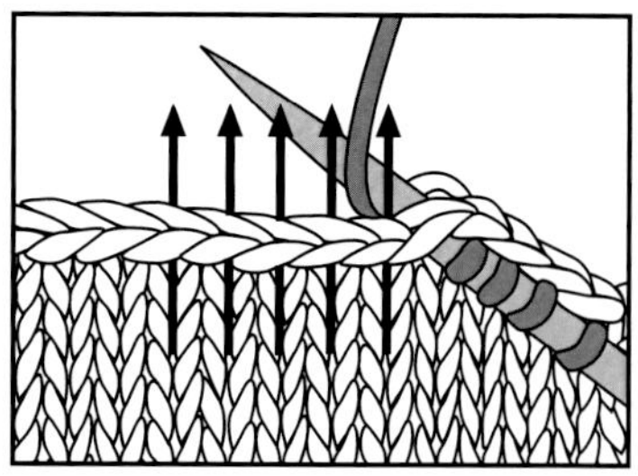

WORKING INTO THE CHAIN

Insert the needle into the back ridge of each chain *(Fig. 14)*.

Fig. 14

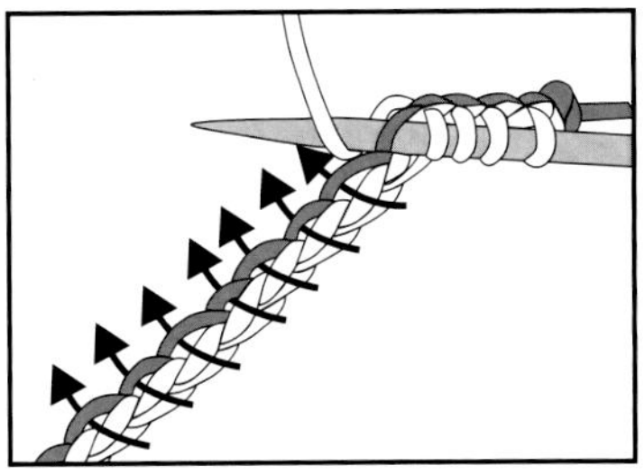

3-NEEDLE BIND OFF

Holding pieces with **right** sides together and needles parallel to each other, insert a third needle as if to **knit** into the first stitch on the front needle **and** into the first stitch on the back needle *(Fig. 15)*. Knit these two stitches together and slip them off the needle. ★ Knit the next stitch on each needle together and slip them off the needle. To bind off, insert the left needle into the first stitch on the right needle and pull the first stitch over the second stitch and off the right needle; repeat from ★ across until all of the stitches on the front needle have been bound off.

Fig. 15

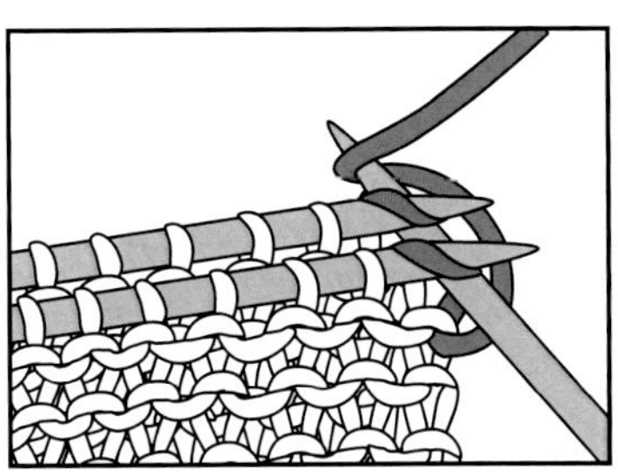

WEAVING SEAMS

With the **right** side of both pieces facing you and edges even, sew through both sides once to secure the seam. Insert the needle under the bar between the first and second stitches on the row and pull the yarn through *(Fig. 16)*. Insert the needle under the next bar on the second side. Repeat from side to side, being careful to match rows. If the edges are different lengths, it may be necessary to insert the needle under two bars at one edge.

Fig. 16

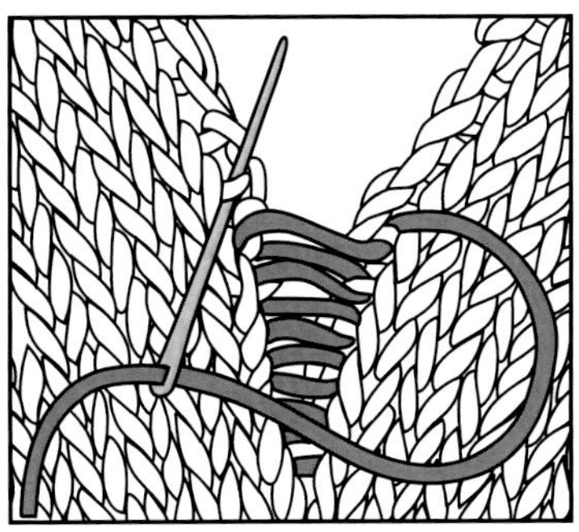

FRINGE

Cut a piece of cardboard 12" (30.5 cm) wide and ½" (12 mm) longer than you want your finished fringe to be. Wind the yarn **loosely** and **evenly** lengthwise around the cardboard until the card is filled, then cut across one end; repeat as needed.

Hold together (half as many strands of yarn as desired for the finished fringe/as many strands as specified in individual instructions); fold in half.

With **wrong** side facing and using a crochet hook, draw the folded end up through a (stitch, space, or row) and pull the loose ends through the folded end *(Fig. 17a)*; draw the knot up **tightly** *(Fig. 17b)*. Repeat, spacing (as desired/as specified in individual instructions).

Lay flat on a hard surface and trim the ends.

Fig. 17a

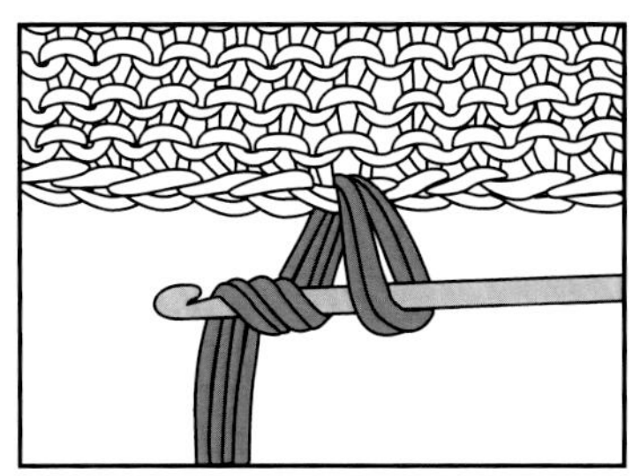

Fig. 17b

YARN INFORMATION

The items in this book were made using a variety of yarns. Any brand of the specific weight of yarn may be used. It is best to refer to the yardage/meters when determining how many balls or skeins to purchase. Remember, to achieve the same look, it is the weight of yarn that is important, not the brand of yarn.

For your convenience, listed below are the specific yarns used to create our photography models. Because yarn manufacturers make frequent changes to their product lines, you may sometimes find it necessary to use a substitute yarn or to search for the discontinued product at alternate suppliers (locally or online).

BABY CARDI

Red Heart® With Love®
#1711 Cameo

SAMPLER CARDI

Red Heart® Amore™
#6316 Chamomile

HOODIE

Red Heart® Hygge™
#8319 Rust

CROP TOP

Lion Brand® 24/7 Cotton®
#149 Silver

We have made every effort to ensure that these instructions are accurate and complete. We cannot, however, be responsible for human error, typographical mistakes, or variations in individual work.

Production Team: Project Manager - Linda A. Daley; Instructional/ Technical Editor - Joan Beebe; Graphic Artist - Angela Ormsby Stark; Photo Stylist - Lori Wenger; and Photographer - Jason Masters.

Meet Melissa Leapman

Makers all over the world know the joy of creating beautiful and useful items using their own hands. With fashion houses in my hometown of New York City currently featuring lots of trendy lace garments, particularly in super hot yarns, it's time to get your lace on!

Although lace patterns might appear especially complicated, they're actually easy and fun to knit. The patterns are created by working a balance of YO increases and simple decreases. (Finally, a reason to make intentional holes in your knitting!)

In this book, I'll walk you through all the basics from beginning to end, from casting on to binding off. Clear photos will show you exactly how to do everything, and the 4 projects will allow you to practice and showcase your new skills.

Every pattern is written in both text and chart form. Some knitters prefer the visual presentation of charts while others like the explicit words. In this book, the choice is yours!

My recent book, *Knitting Modular Shawls* (Storey Publishing, 2018) explores the beauty of lace shawls and wraps for beginners and avid knitters. But *Fashionable Lace* lets you discover other types of lace projects.

There's magic in every ball of yarn. Let's add a few YOs to a little bit of creativity and watch things get really fun Find me on Instagram as Melissa.Leapman and on Ravelry as MelissaLeapman. I look forward to knitting with you!